Accounting, Finance, Sustainability, Governance & Fraud: Theory and Application

Series Editor

Kıymet Tunca Çalıyurt, Iktisadi ve Idari Bilimler Fakultes, Trakya University Balkan Yerleskesi, Edirne, Turkey

This Scopus indexed series acts as a forum for book publications on current research arising from debates about key topics that have emerged from global economic crises during the past several years. The importance of governance and the will to deal with corruption, fraud, and bad practice, are themes featured in volumes published in the series. These topics are not only of concern to businesses and their investors, but also to governments and supranational organizations, such as the United Nations and the European Union. Accounting, Finance, Sustainability, Governance & Fraud: Theory and Application takes on a distinctive perspective to explore crucial issues that currently have little or no coverage. Thus the series integrates both theoretical developments and practical experiences to feature themes that are topical, or are deemed to become topical within a short time. The series welcomes interdisciplinary research covering the topics of accounting, auditing, governance, and fraud.

More information about this series at https://link.springer.com/bookseries/13615

İlknur Kumkale

Organizational Mastery

The Impact of Strategic Leadership and Organizational Ambidexterity on Organizational Agility

Springer

İlknur Kumkale
Faculty of Economics
and Administrative Sciences
Trakya University
Edirne, Turkey

ISSN 2509-7873 ISSN 2509-7881 (electronic)
Accounting, Finance, Sustainability, Governance & Fraud: Theory and Application
ISBN 978-981-16-7581-2 ISBN 978-981-16-7582-9 (eBook)
https://doi.org/10.1007/978-981-16-7582-9

This Springer imprint is published by the registered company Springer Nature Singapore Pte Ltd.
The registered company address is: 152 Beach Road, #21-01/04 Gateway East, Singapore 189721, Singapore

To my dear mother and father...

My reasons for existence,

who laid the foundations I need to stand strong in my life,

To my dear husband Bülent...

I have always felt his support by my side since the day I started my academic life.

and

To my dear daughter Çıdam...

From the moment she was born, her presence gives me strength in everything I do.

Contents

1 Organizational Ambidexterity 1
1.1 Introduction 2
1.2 The Concept of Ambidexterity 4
1.3 Dimensions of Organizational Ambidexterity 9
1.3.1 Structural Ambidexterity 9
1.3.2 Contextual Ambidexterity 13
1.4 Ambidexterity Management Strategies 15
1.5 The Role of Leadership in Implementing Ambidexterity Strategies 17
References 19

2 Strategic Leadership 23
2.1 Introduction 23
2.2 Strategic Leadership Models 26
2.2.1 John Adair's "The Three Circles Model" 26
2.2.2 "Nine-Point Strategic Leadership Model" of Davies and Davies 27
2.2.3 The Strategic Leadership Model of Ülgen and Mirze Addressing the "Hard and Soft Factors" 28
2.2.4 Five Dimensional Strategic Leadership Model of Pisapia 29
2.3 Dimensions of Strategic Leadership 30
2.3.1 Managerial Strategic Leadership 30
2.3.2 Transformational Strategic Leadership 31
2.3.3 Political Strategic Leadership 32
2.3.4 Ethical Strategic Leadership 32
2.3.5 Communicative Strategic Leadership 33
References 34

3 Organizational Agility 37
3.1 Introduction 37
3.2 Conceptual Framework 38
3.2.1 Agility 38
3.2.2 Strategic Agility 39
3.2.3 Organizational Characteristics of Agile Organization 41
3.3 Dimensions of Organizational Agility 44
3.3.1 Competency 44
3.3.2 Flexibility 45
3.3.3 Responsiveness 45
3.3.4 Quickness 46
3.4 The Effects of Agility in Creating Competitive Advantage 47
References 50

4 Field Study to Evaluate the Effect of Strategic Leadership and Organizational Ambidexterity on Organizational Agility 53
4.1 The Purpose and Importance of the Research 54
4.2 Brief Theoretical Background on the Relationship of Research Variables 54
4.2.1 Research-Based Dynamic Capabilities Theory that Forms the Basis of Research 55
4.2.2 Organizational Ambidexterity—Strategic Leadership 55
4.2.3 Organizational Agility—Strategic Leadership 57
4.3 Population and Sample 59
4.4 Constraints of the Research 60
4.5 Data Collection Method and Scales Used in the Research 60
4.5.1 Strategic Leadership Scale 61
4.5.2 Organizational Ambidexterity Scale 61
4.5.3 Organizational Agility Scale 62
4.6 Research Model and Hypotheses 62
4.7 Structural Equation Modeling Assumptions 63
4.8 Findings of the Research 66
4.8.1 Socio-demographical Characteristics of the Respondents 67
4.8.2 Analysis and Findings for Scales 69
4.8.3 Testing the Research Model 88
4.9 Discussion 96
References 109

Appendix: A 113

Appendix: B 123

Index 127

About the Author

Assoc. Prof. İlknur Kumkale She graduated from Istanbul University Faculty of Economics in 1984. She completed her master's degree in 1995 and her doctorate in 1998 at the Trakya University Institute of Science, Department of Agricultural Economics.

Following her studies at various levels in the private sector between 1984 and 1994, she worked as Research Assistant in the Department of Business Administration and Organization at Trakya University Faculty of Economics and Administrative Sciences and as Lecturer in the Accounting Program of Trakya University Malkara Vocational School between 1995 and 1999.

Between 1999 and 2009, she worked as Assistant Professor at Trakya University Malkara Vocational School as Director of Vocational School. In 2009, she started working at Trakya University Faculty of Economics and Administrative Sciences in the Department of Business Administration and Organization as Assistant Professor. At the same time, she was appointed as Founding Director of Trakya University Keşan Yusuf Çapraz Applied Sciences School. Completing the establishment of the college with the significant support of local people, institutions and local government, she continued this mission until August 2012.

She received the title of Associate Professor in Management and Strategy in 2015. Currently, she works in the Department of Management and Organization under the Department of Business Administration of the Faculty of Economics and Administrative Sciences and teaches various courses (business administration, strategic management, etc.) in the undergraduate, graduate and doctorate programs. In addition to the ongoing theses under her supervision, many master projects, three PhDs and seven master theses have been completed. She also has articles published in national and international journals and papers presented in congresses. She has 12 book chapters published by National and International Publishers and one chapter Turkish translation in a book (TUBA/Turkey Academy of Sciences, 2012 Year of Notable Author Award/Honorable Mention was awarded, edited by Prof. Dr. Ugur Yozgat, Laudon, KC & J.P. Laudon Management Information Systems Managing the Digital Firm). In addition, she has two books as a single author (Examination of General Business and Women's Entrepreneurship in Terms of Strategic Leadership

Competencies); one book she edited (Woman's Business Life and Ethics) and one project book with co-authors.

She was awarded the "Woman Entrepreneur of the Year" Award by Keşan Chamber of Commerce and Industry in 2013 and is a member of the High Advisory Board of the same institution. She holds the memberships of several organizations like Faculty of Economics Alumni Association, Turkey Charity Association, Turkish Association of University Women, Edirne/Kesan Women Entrepreneurs Board Member, Trakya University Quality and Strategy Development Group, Department of Business AACSB Commission (Strategy & Quality & Ethics Compliance). She is Certified Public Accountant with the License. Kumkale is married and has a daughter.

List of Figures

Fig. 2.1 Strategic Leadership Pyram ... 25
Fig. 2.2 Broad functions of strategic leadership ... 27
Fig. 2.3 Davies and Davies's strategic leadership model ... 28
Fig. 2.4 The strategic leadership model of Ülgen and Mirze ... 28
Fig. 3.1 Relationship between learning and core competence ... 41
Fig. 4.1 Conceptual model of the research ... 63
Fig. 4.2 Gender distribution of the managers participating in the survey ... 69
Fig. 4.3 Age distribution of the managers participating in the survey ... 70
Fig. 4.4 Education level distribution of the managers participating in the survey ... 70
Fig. 4.5 Tenure of the managers participating in the survey in the company ... 71
Fig. 4.6 Tenure of the managers participating in the survey in the profession ... 72
Fig. 4.7 Managerial levels of the managers participating in the survey ... 72
Fig. 4.8 Sector in which the company operates ... 73
Fig. 4.9 Companies according to their scale ... 73
Fig. 4.10 Number of in-service activities the respondent managers participated related to their profession ... 74
Fig. 4.11 Strategic leadership CFA path diagram ... 84
Fig. 4.12 Organizational ambidexterity CFA path diagram ... 87
Fig. 4.13 Organizational agility CFA path diagram ... 90
Fig. 4.14 Research model ... 93
Fig. 4.15 Structural equation model ... 93
Fig. 4.16 The effect of transformational leadership on organizational agility dimensions ... 104
Fig. 4.17 The effect of organizational Ambidexterity dimensions on organizational agility dimensions ... 105

Fig. 4.18 The effect of political strategic leadership on organizational ambidexterity 106
Fig. 4.19 The effect of managerial strategic leadership on organizational ambidexterity dimensions 107
Fig. 4.20 The effect of managerial strategic leadership on organizational agility through organizational ambidexterity 107
Fig. 4.21 The effect of political strategic leadership on organizational agility through organizational ambidexterity 108

List of Tables

Table 1.1 Organizational ambidexterity approaches 10
Table 1.2 Differences between contextual ambidexterity and structural ambidexterity 15
Table 3.1 Organizational features of agile enterprises 43
Table 3.2 Characteristics of agile workforce 44
Table 4.1 Dimensions of strategic leadership scale 61
Table 4.2 Dimensions of structural ambidexterity scale 61
Table 4.3 Dimensions of contextual ambidexterity scale 62
Table 4.4 Dimensions of organizational agility scale 62
Table 4.5 Research hypotheses 64
Table 4.6 Socio-demographical characteristics of the Respondents 68
Table 4.7 Descriptive statistics on the Items of the strategic leadership scale 75
Table 4.8 Descriptive statistics on the items of the organizational ambidexterity 78
Table 4.9 Descriptive statistics on the Items of the organizational agility 80
Table 4.10 Reliability analysis results of the scales used in the study 82
Table 4.11 Significance levels of strategic leadership confirmatory factor analysis 85
Table 4.12 Confirmatory factor analysis fit values of the strategic leadership scale 86
Table 4.13 Significance levels of confirmatory factor analysis related to organizational ambidexterity scale 88
Table 4.14 Confirmatory factor analysis fit values of the organizational ambidexterity scale 89
Table 4.15 Significance levels of confirmatory factor analysis related to organizational agility scale 91
Table 4.16 Confirmatory factor analysis fit values of organizational agility scale 92
Table 4.17 Regression weights 94

Table 4.18 Squared R^2 multiple correlations 95
Table 4.19 Standardized direct effects 97
Table 4.20 Fit values of structural equation model 98
Table 4.21 Standardized indirect effects 99
Table 4.22 Standardized indirect effects 100
Table 4.23 Indirect effects—lower bounds 101
Table 4.24 Indirect effects—upper bounds 102
Table 4.25 Supported hypotheses according to analysis results 103

Chapter 1
Organizational Ambidexterity

Abstract It is not possible for businesses to implement their strategic plans without changing them as the organizations that operate in a constantly changing environment and are not independent and nisolated from their environment. In the strategic management of organizations, it is important to organize and store all kinds of information (qualitative and quantitative) obtained under uncertain and variable conditions, to predict risks, and to take effective decisions by evaluating all resources and opportunities. Therefore, while the organizations need to look for most efficient ways of benefiting the resources they have, they ought to evaluate the opportunities around them. Even though it requires opposing strategies in organizational management, being able to use these two approaches at the same time is expressed with the concept of ambidexterity as an organizational capability. When organizational ambidexterity is considered with its structural dimension; it is the ability of reshaping the resources and capabilities of the enterprise according to changing conditions (exploitation), within the same process, by acquiring new resources and developing new skills (exploration) to evaluate the opportunities that occur in the environment, that is, the ability to carry out this process together. When it is considered with its contextual dimension; it is the ability to carrying out the activities within the organization in harmony (alignment) on one side, on the other side, it is the ability to restructure its activities in business units to meet the changing expectations and needs of consumers (adaptability). In this context, organizations with ambidexterity, which can be considered as a dynamic capability, can ensure sustainable competitive advantage by increasing their organizational performance both in the short run and in the long run. This study is conducted to research the impact of strategic leadership and organizational ambidexterity skills on the strategic agility of the organization by examining the literature on the subject. Furthermore, the role of organizational ambidexterity in the impact of strategic leadership on strategic agility of the organization is investigated. This study consists of four parts. In the first part, ambidexterity concept is discussed, and then the issue of organizational ambidexterity is explained with its dimensions. Exploratory and beneficiary innovation abilities and also adaptability and customization are examined as sub dimensions. In the second part, strategic leadership issue is being explained. Firstly it is handled conceptually; then follows the review in five dimensions as managerial

İ. Kumkale, *Organizational Mastery*, Accounting, Finance, Sustainability, Governance & Fraud: Theory and Application, https://doi.org/10.1007/978-981-16-7582-9_1

strategic leadership, transformational strategic leadership, political strategic leadership, communicative strategic leadership and ethical strategic leadership. The third part focuses on strategic agility. The occurrence of agility concept, the concept of organizational agility and the importance of agility are explained; and agility in organizations with its competence, flexibility, responsiveness and speed dimensions is discussed. In the fourth part, place is given to field study, and the results are evaluated by analyzing the data obtained from the questionnaires applied to the managers of large and medium-sized enterprises. Organizational ambidexterity concept came up with Duncan's study he made in 1976 (Kauppila in Strateg Org 8(4):283–312, 2010). Successful organizations being versatile and coherent in management of today's business demands (Duncan in J Pers Soc Psychol 34:590, 1976; Tushman and O'Reilly in Calif Manage Rev 38:8–30, 1996) along with them displaying behavioral models adaptable to the changes that may occur in their environment in the future (Gibson and Birkinshaw in Acad Manage J 47(2):209–226, 2004) became a prominent subject. Such kinds of organizations are those, skilled and effectively adaptable to changes in their internal and external environments simultaneously, namely the organizations having ambidexterity competence. Therefore, the study of Duncan generated a stimulating effect and it has become an issue of increasing interest of the researchers working on management, strategy and organization (Raisch and Birkinshaw in J Manage 34(3):375–409, 2008). However, it seems that, more studies are needed.

Keywords Ambidexterity · Exploitation · Exploration · Alignment · Adaptability

1.1 Introduction

> The best way to predict your future is to create it.
>
> Peter F. Drucker

The environment that organizations are in is becoming more dynamic every day, and it is not so easy for companies to adapt to this speed and dynamism. Being able to perceive the expectations of customers correctly and respond as quickly as possible causes companies and their leaders to reconsider and question their talents and competencies from a different perspective. This situation brings into question the ability of companies of all sizes to carry out their research activities simultaneously, while benefiting from their own competencies. In other saying; planning both their present and future, as well as balancing their attention and resource allocation for their sustainability activities, become even more important (Sinha 2015). The necessity for rapid change and transformation shortens the average time, that companies maintain their competitive advantage, making it difficult for them to gain long-term competitive advantage—in high-speed competitive environments (Barreto 2010). The competition conditions of today, depending to the development of information and communication technologies and hence the increase of mobility and variability, causes competition go beyond national borders and take place simultaneously in the global environment, which makes it necessary for businesses to be agile. Businesses can gain competitive advantage by means of rapidly responding to the demands and expectations of their customers with their agile business models they will implement besides the agile production techniques and methods they will use. Therefore their goods and/or services can reach consumers quickly. Businesses that can quickly perceive the changes occurring in their environment-take measures and implement the necessary practices before their competitors are agile businesses that can maintain their sustainability and thus increase their lifetimes above the averages. Strategic agility means that, organizations can effectively manage their internal environments, while following their external environment with strong foresight and sensitive perception; performing flexible applications and maintaining their strategic sensitivity without losing speed. In other words, it means managing the change and responding rapidly (Kumkale 2016). The ability of organizations to adapt to change, and be managed in unpredictable environments require strategic leadership management skills. To form an interaction of the strategic leaders between behavioral and cultural differences and at the same time in uncertainty to display personal and visionary skills that may affect the behaviors, thoughts and feelings of the people they work with (Peters 2001) becomes important under these circumstances. Global business competition can not only be interpreted as the competition between company and company or product and product; but also between mentality and mentality, and managerial structure to managerial structure (Hamel and Prahald 1993). With respect to the performance efficiency of the strategic leaders business contexts are also important. Competent strategic leaders also create the context in which stakeholders can perform at their highest efficiency (Kets de Vries 1995; Raza and Murad 2014).

For organizations, in order to present the behavioral models required by the changes in global environment and take advantages in competition, it is important that, while they are making the best use of their resources, they take their places in the market with their production of innovative and different goods and services as well. The businesses which are capable of generating solutions for the prospective needs and capable of rapidly and effective responding to unexpected opportunities—agile businesses—(Nelson and Harvey 1995) will gain competitive advantage in this subject. Strategic leaders, on the other hand, are the people having competencies capable to activate internal and external dynamics with a visionary perspective by perceiving and evaluating the opportunities and threats in the external environment of organizations in the most accurate and fastest way.

Sometimes the threats the organizations come across turn into a crisis; not only may cause a single organization to be affected, but may cause global effects. Whatever the reason may be, many different crises have been experienced in the past and today and will continue to be experienced in the future, too. However, while some organizations experience negative effects of a crisis; some others manage to turn crises into an opportunity.

Strategic management is to make decisions in environment of uncertainties and why some of the organizations become much more successful in comparison to others is one of the fundamental research areas. The extent of the strategic management skills applied in an organization in a sense can be considered as the answer to this question

(Hitt and Ireland 2002). Starting from this point, it is possible to say that opportunities and threats show up simultaneously for every business; however, whichever business is more agile in the market, that one benefits from these opportunities at first, and also that business perceives the threats first (Kumkale 2016).

As known the corona virus, which started to be seen in Wuhan City of China in late December 2019, has effects having spread beyond the borders of the country, and is declared as "Global Pandemic" by the World Health Organization on March 12, 2020. Although this disease initially made itself felt as a health crisis, later on by spreading worldwide, it was not left only as a health crisis, and transformed into a global crisis with the economic and social effects it created. This period caused organizations all over the world to reconsider their ways of doing business and adapt these to conditions prevailing (Demirel et al. 2020). The year 2020 we left behind, had been a year when organizations endeavored to be agile and maintain their sustainability. When we think about this example recently experienced, it is possible to state that businesses with organizational agility turned this crisis into an opportunity and gained advantage in competition. Businesses that maintain their sustainability are those that increase their core competencies, develop and use them properly, benefit the opportunities of the external environment, and eliminate its threats. Effective management of this process requires efficient strategic leadership skills.

1.2 The Concept of Ambidexterity

Ambidexterity originates from the combination of the words "ambae", meaning both, and "dexterit/as" meaning skill, and the word "ambidextrous" is used as a metaphor for people who can use both right and left hand at the same time with the same skill (Bodwell and Chermark 2010: 196). This, Latin-based English word started taking place in the field literature as a subject of great interest in recent years.

Organizational theorists have recently adopted this metaphor to describe versatile organizations, stating that such versatile firms can search out new opportunities with equal skill as well as being able to benefit from their existing competencies (Lubatkin et al. 2006).

Ambidexterity metaphor is used by the researchers to express the capabilities of an organization, on one side exploitation (benefit from) the present resources and on the other side to manage the exploration (search out) activities to survive today, gain superiority and secure the future by creating sustainable growth potential of the organization in the future, that is, in a sense of capability of paying double attention of the organization. Since the requirements of both activities are different and also counter to each other, it is denoted that to manage this couple is not so easy (Sinha 2015).

The scope of exploitation concept includes productivity, preferences and choices made in business resources, practices and implementation activities. Explorative/research activities on the other hand, state to explore or search out the unbeknown for obtaining much more yields for the organization. Here, the activities such as taking risks, searching out and innovations are talked about (March 1991). Therefore, the activities of exploitation and exploration may require different organization structures, strategies and contexts in principle. Some scientists suggest that there is an interchange between structuring the organization to take advantage of existing capabilities and structuring it to discover new ones. For this reason, in contemporary management theory, firms are often forced to focus on exploitation or exploratory activities by presenting organizational facts in terms of separate, opposite categories.

March, in his 1991 article on the subject, contrary to these, argued that organizations should both make full use of their resources and be adapted to exploratory works (Raisch and Birkinshaw 2008). Managers and organizations will surely be in a dilemma in practice, they may need to eliminate their increasing efforts in strategy, structure and adaptation periodically in the short run to build a new organization in the long run (Tushman and O'Reilly 1996).

When the literature is reviewed, it is seen that, in many studies conducted over time, the tendency has a multiple perspective towards the necessity of maintaining the managerial tensions arising from the continuation of contradictory activities in organizations and the simultaneous or sequential management of such activities (Sinha 2015). In the literature, when it comes to managing or balancing dichotomies such as simultaneous application and balancing of exploratory and resource exploitation activities, stimulated and autonomous strategy processes, incremental and discontinuous innovation, research, and cessation/stability, different qualifications have been used. In spite of the fact that these qualifications are different, mainly the phenomenon of ambidexterity is referred to and is cited as a critical precursor of company performance (Raisch and Birkinshaw 2008).

Raisch and Birkinshaw (2008), from 1991 and then on by reviewing the key studies published in leading management journals such as Academy of Management Journal, Academy of Management Review, Administrative Science Quarterly, Journal of Management, Journal of Management Studies, Organization Science and Strategic Management Journal and by evaluating many discussion papers, have developed a framework that integrates the precursors of organizational versatility, environmental impacts, moderators and performance results. In their work, the contradictions between exploitation and exploration and the need to reconcile the two orientations are discussed within the contexts of *organizational learning, technological innovation, organizational adaptation, strategic management and organizational design*. Also Sinha (2015) in his research stated that, in the previous studies contradictory activities should be carried out in organizations and such activities were carried out sometimes simultaneously, sometimes sequentially, and various tensions were experienced in this process. He stated that, the simultaneous use of exploitation and exploration is basically referred to ambidexterity skills and discussed together with the issues of *organizational theory* (Burns and Stalker 1961; Thompson 1967. Citiced by Spender and Kessler 1995), *technological innovation* (Tushman and Anderson

1986; Anderson and Tushman 1990; Smith and Tushman 2005), *organizational adaptation* (Tushman and Romanelli 1985; Tushman and O'Reilly 1996), *organizational learning* (Senge 1990; March 1991; Levinthal and March 1993) and *strategic management* (Bugelman 1991, 2002; Ghemawat and Ricart Costa 1993; Hamel and Prahalad 1993; Sanchez and Mahoney 1996), and it has been shown that this is a critical precursor of company performance.

These topics (Raisch and Birkinshaw 2008) will be explained briefly below, and their relationship to organizational ambidexterity will be discussed.

Organizational learning: In literature, it is seen that there are two different points of view with respect to exploitation and explorative approaches. According to the opinion of a group of researchers; while only re-use of existing knowledge is a matter of exploitation approach, organizational learning and all learning types are valid for the exploratory approach. The opinion of the other group is more in line with the views of March (1991) and it is seen that, this opinion focuses on the type or degree of learning, rather than the presence or absence of learning (Raisch and Birkinshaw 2008).

Despite the differences between the two learning processes, academicians thought that a balanced combination of the two learning styles was necessary for long-term organizational success (Gupta et al. 2006; Levinthal and March 1993; March 1991) quoted by Raisch and Birkinshaw (2008). It is also stated in the studies that learning mechanisms play a key role in dynamic abilities (Grant 1996), and that without learning mechanisms, information sources cannot effectively transform into dynamic skills (Chien and Tsai 2012). According to the study conducted by Smith and Prieto (2008), it is possible to explain the exploratory learning approach with dynamic abilities and the beneficiary approach on a knowledge-based perspective.

According to Mom et al. (2007), the top-down flow of information from top managers to down is positively associated with exploitation. On the other hand horizontal and bottom-up information flow from equal level peers and lower hierarchical levels are positively associated with exploratory. Findings show that the more a manager acquires a top-down and horizontal or bottom-up flow of information, the higher the levels of discovery and exploitation the manager is involved in.

Technological innovation: When the innovation and technological innovation examined, in general two different kinds of innovations are pointed out: Progressive/incremental/increasing innovation and radical/revolutionary/discontinuous innovation. *Incremental innovation* is generally used in the meaning of introducing an innovation by using existing technology and methods. Incremental innovation represents relatively small adaptations of present products and business concepts. The innovations made in this way are either improvement of a present thing or reconstruction of an existing thing to serve another purpose. In other ways, they can be defined as the innovations made within certain limits (Luecke 2008). On the contrary, *radical innovation* refers to fundamental changes that lead to the transition from existing products, technologies or concepts to completely new ones (Raisch and Birkinshaw 2008). Clayton Christensen has used the concept of *disruptive technology* to describe radical innovation that has the power to potentially disrupt the business models of existing institutions or industries. Disruptive technologies take the places of existing technologies and accelerate the fall of those companies dependent on those technologies (Luecke 2008). Tushman and O'Reilly (1996), state that an organization's ability to follow both incremental and discontinuous innovation at the same time is the ability of ambidexterity, and these kinds of organizations shelter more than one contradictory structure, process and culture. Colbert (2004), on the other hand, in another saying argues that the interaction between exploratory and exploitation approach reflects a complex ability that provides an additional corporate advantage beyond the benefits and returns provided by both innovation activities separately.

Organizational adaptation: There are many scholars who have argued that to ensure a long-term success in organizations require an organizational balance between continuity and change. The common thought expressed; in case of continuity is ignored and only innovations are cared for, too much or too radical act of change can create organizational chaos; on the contrary, only the emphasis of order and continuity can lead to inaction (Huy 2002; Levinthal and March 1993; Sastry 1997). While some researchers argue that there is a need for regular and rhythmic organizational change through time flow (Brown and Eisenhardt 1997), some others argue that, managers came central position to "mediating between convergence forces and forces of change" (Tushman and Romanelli 1985). Convergence in short and simple terms; is expressed as coming close of both contents and the channels carrying them to each other (Geçkin Onat 2017). It was argued that, senior management is mostly the main driver of discontinuous change, while the middle management supports gradual change (Floyd and Woolridge 1996; Shrivastava 1986) in the meantime they facilitate organizational adaptation through emotional balance of continuity and change (Huy 2002), (Raisch and Birkinshaw 2008). Abatecola (2012) on the other hand, questioned that, whether the relationship between organizational adaptation and ambidexterity experience is innovation adaptation styles or "exaptation" oriented. Cattani (2005, 2006 and 2008) and Dew and Sarasvathy (2007) have argued that, in recent years, an increasing number of management academicians have begun to use the foundations of biological studies—exaptation—to understand which mechanisms can break product and process innovations, as well as examine which mechanisms can promote radical technological or organizational change.

Strategic management: It is emphasized that, the pressure between seeking innovations that can generate leverage effect and exploitation the existing capabilities to create competitive advantage is a key strategic challenge in creating competitive advantage (Hamel and Prahald 1993). It is seen that Burgelman (1991, 2002) proposes the strategy formulation in different ways as stimulated strategic processes that reduce differentiation and autonomous strategic processes that increase diversity. Promoted, namely stimulated processes are related to initiatives that fall within the scope of the organization's existing strategy and build on existing knowledge. Autonomous processes, on the other hand, related to the initiatives arising outside the scope of the existing strategy and involve the creation of new competencies. Burgelman in his 2002 dated article associated the stimulated strategic processes with utilization approach and autonomous strategy processes with exploration.

The features inherent in strategic management such as being future-oriented, making a gain above average earnings, managing with alternatives, and gaining advantage in competition require the organization to utilize its competencies in the best manner and to be ready and strong against opportunities and threats in its external environment.

Both types of strategic processes for this reason compete for scarce resources. Being in the topic for company leaders to share preferences and resources for both processes, and Burgelman (1991) proposes that, a combination of the two strategic processes may be the most beneficial practice.

Ghemawat and Ricart Costa (1993) mention of dynamic efficiency as the improvement of existing products, processes and capabilities, while dynamic efficiency as the development of innovations and state that, there is an organizational exchange between these two strategic processes.

While some authors state that successful companies have the capacity to sustain a mixture of competence enhancement and competence development activities (Citiced by Guiette and Vandenbempt 2014), Cingöz and Akdoğan (2015) express that the first condition of implementing the organizational ambidexterity strategy is top managers having strategic consciousness.

For managers, accepting the changes in the external environment which will create some new opportunities and threats for them and hence showing the necessary willingness and make arrangements to adapt to change is of vital importance.

Organization theory: When the history of organization management is reviewed, it is seen that organizational theory experts have been working on the operation of organizational structures that have both efficiency and flexibility for many years. Burns and Stalker (1961) mention about two principal organizational structures; mechanical organizational structure and organic organizational structure. Mechanical organizations are the structures dominated by centralization and hierarchy, with most decisions taken by senior management. These type of structures support stability and efficiency. On the other hand, in organic organizations, the decision-making mechanism has a decentralized structure. They are autonomous structures used in organizations that are encountered in unstable, dynamic environments and need to adapt quickly to change, and they support flexibility. While Thompson (1967) argued that the preferences of organizations between efficiency and flexibility is a "management paradox" (Tan and Wang 2010) and Duncan (1976) stated that, organizations need both of these two structures, and they need an organic structure to create innovations and also they need a mechanical structure to implement them.

In fact, despite the paradoxical difficulties of both structures taking place together in the same organization, there are many studies proposing that organizations having ambidexterity are the organizations that can achieve this; also many researchers state that despite the difficulties, it is important that two structures coexist in harmony in an organization.

1.3 Dimensions of Organizational Ambidexterity

As the structure of organizational ambidexterity attract the attention of organizational theorists, studies on this subject began to increase. Looking at the studies in the literature, it seems that in general a consensus has been arrived on the organizations developing ambidexterity strategies and has management skills in this direction, both have the ability to use existing competencies and to explore new opportunities increase the performance and competitiveness of the company. However, beyond these points, it is possible to mention that there are some disagreements about the nature of ambidexterity and there are some important uncertainties (Cao et al. 2009). In Table 1.1, displays the dimensions, in which researchers consider and examine organizational ambidexterity.

1.3.1 Structural Ambidexterity

From a strategic management perspective, all organizations profit oriented or not are revenue-oriented and all want to be sustainable. At the same time, there is competition always existing in all fields for all organizations. Therefore, every organization gives efforts to gain advantage in competition. In order to achieve these goals, they determine their assets and competencies with the internal analyses they make and the opportunities and threats they may possibly encounter with external analyses. When considered on the basis of profit oriented organizations, it is clear that organizations will want to mobilize all their opportunities in order to gain competitive advantage and obtain a profit above the average. However, their resources may sometimes fail to meet their strategic goals, and this situation may force the managers of the organization to make choices about the decisions they will make and their investments they will actualize. Since, the management activities such as organizational structures, division of labor, coordination and supervision have a guiding effect on achieving the organizational goals. It will affect the processes and results in many issues from determining the individuals who will participate in the decision making processes to the shaping of standard procedures and organizational actions. While these decisions are taken, the goals of the organization gain importance and different structures can be moved off. While some organizations aim to be successful by focusing on assets and competencies (exploitation) and developing them, others aim to develop by focusing on different and new activities (exploratory) that they did not have before. While these two approaches require structuring in different directions, trying to implement both structures in the same organization requires a separate skill, which is expressed as structural ambidexterity competence.

Structural ambidexterity is the ability to manage the opposite and contradictory elements in an organization simultaneously in a balanced manner. In other words, it is the integration of different abilities, systems, processes and cultural characteristics around a common strategic intention. Therefore, structural ambidexterity requires

Table 1.1 Organizational ambidexterity approaches

Researchers	Year of the research	Their approaches to ambidexterity
March	1991	Exploration and exploitation capability
Benner and Tushman	2003	Exploration and exploitation capability
Birkinshaw and Gibson	2004	Adaptability and alignment capability
He and Wong	2004	Exploration and exploitation capability
Auh ve Menguc	2005	Exploration and exploitation capability
Gupta et al.	2006	Exploration and exploitation capability
Lubatkin et al.	2006	Exploration and exploitation capability
Bierly and Daly	2007	Exploration and exploitation capability
Menguc and Auh	2008	Exploration and exploitation Capability
Raish and Birkinshaw	2008	Exploration and Exploitation capability
Chen and Katila	2008	Exploration and exploitation capability
Cao et al.	2009	Exploration and exploitation capability
Akdoğan et al.	2009	Exploration and exploitation capability
Giridharadas	2009	Exploration and exploitation capability
Jansen et al.	2009	Exploration and exploitation capability
Mom vd	2009	Exploration and exploitation capability
Andriopoulos and Lewis	2009	Exploration and exploitation capability
Bodwell and Chermack	2010	Exploration and exploitation capability
Hughes vd	2010	Exploration and exploitation capability
Turner et al.	2011	Exploration and exploitation capability
Lee and Huang	2012	Exploration and exploitation capability
Chang and Hughes	2012	Exploration and exploitation capability
Boumgarden et al.	2012	Exploration and exploitation capability
O'Reilly and Tushman	2013	Exploration and exploitation capability
Clercq et al.	2013	Adaptability and alignment capability
Kortman et al.	2014	Adaptability and alignment capability
Tansley et al.	2014	Exploration and exploitation capability
Javier et al.	2014	Exploration and exploitation capability
Fındıklı Afacan and Pınar	2014	Exploration and Exploitation Capability
Paliokaite and Pacesa	2015	Exploration and exploitation capability
Sinha	2015	Exploration and exploitation capability
Çekmecelioğlu et al.	2018	Exploration and exploitation capability
Bakan et al.	2019	Exploration and exploitation capability

Source It has been prepared based on studies of Bakan and Sezer (2017) and Özbebek Tunç (2017)

creating different structures for different activities (Birkinshaw and Gibson 2004; O'Reilley and Tushman 2013). March (1991) introduced the concepts of exploitation and exploration to the management literature for the first time, and argued that there are two extremes in the continuity of the organization. According to March, these two concepts contradict each other by their very nature. March stated that there is competition between exploitation and exploration orientations and that the management should endeavor to achieve a certain balance. That is because a one-sided focus on exploitation can improve short-term performance, whereas it can put organizations in a competence trap and organizations may not respond adequately to environmental changes.

Quinn and Cameron (1983) stated that the growth stages of organizations require a focus on rapid expansion (exploitation) and creativity and innovation (exploration), and the ability of the founder delegating the responsibility and control to others also have critical importance on sustaining the growth. Considering the existence of factors such as development of a sense of acting together, having a shared mission, and commitment to the idea of continuation of innovation in the rapid growth period, it is possible to mention that companies undertake exploitation and exploration activities at different stages throughout their life cycles.

1.3.1.1 Exploitation (Beneficiary) Innovation Capability

When exploitation practices are considered with respect to organizational and business strategies; it is stated that, the organizational structure is centralized in the sense of promoting production, synergy and efficiency; the authority is descended from top to bottom and not distributed too much. This situation leads to an increase in organizational rigidity, the formation of a mechanical structure and the preparation of an exploitation environment.

When the present activities of the organization are aimed to improve, "exploitation" is necessary since it yields positive results in the short run (Caroll 2012). This comprises the works performed on incremental improvements in existing goods and services using the existing knowledge in order to meet the needs of the company's present customers. The organizations adopting exploitative activities set their strategies over generating profits by reducing costs and increasing efficiency. Selection and implementation of strategy is shaped by the chosen business model, allocation of budget and the financial targets. For example, if the company as a dominant market player wants to gain competitive advantages, it should focus on efficiency (exploitation/benefit) and cost leadership based on centralized decision making (Blarr 2011. Cited by Özbebek Tunç 2017).

1.3.1.2 Exploration Innovation Capability

Research activities focus on radical innovation (Blarr 2011. Cited by Özbebek Tunç 2017), change and the future (Smith and Tushman 2005), exploring the unexplored

(March 1991) to meet the needs of potential customers rather than existing customers. Businesses that strategically aim innovation, environmental compliance and growth, labor to acquire new knowledge beside existing knowledge.

For businesses that focus on exploring (discovering) innovations and shifting their activities towards this direction it is possible to dissipate their resources in a short period of time on these efforts, the return of which are to be obtained in an uncertain time. This is because the returns of such studies are generally lagged (Cited by Gözen 2018). Even if the innovative works create new possibilities, failure of the first outcomes may cause temporary decreases in performance (Gözen 2018), and cost increases. Hence, not every business may prefer to proceed in this way. The businesses preferring explorative activities are searchers; they give emphasize on diversification, adopt long-range perspective and have elastic structure. Meanwhile it is possible to say that, this kind of a work structure may add new skills to the organizations. If a company's strategic purpose is to be excellent by means of constantly catching new opportunities and expanding its existing markets, it should focus on flexibility, which requires taking decentralized decisions (Blarr 2011. Cited by Özbebek Tunç 2017).

Structural Ambidexterity suggests for enterprises having organizational ambidexterity building up different specific units or structures that will carry out exploitation and exploration activities and equipping these structures with relevant incentive systems and control mechanisms. Since the task and authority to ensure the overall harmony and coordination of the enterprise is under the top management, it is expected that the top management has the ability to decide between the strategies that support exploitation and exploration activities (Dupouet et al. 2013. Cited by Özbebek Tunç 2017). Dupouet et al. have stated in their study published in 2013 that, at the company they examined, ambidexterity skill is obtained by means of a procedure in which all organization got involved. For example; anywhere in the organization ideas are generated, then channelized to certain exploration teams, and after being developed and improved further herein, they are presented for evaluation of top management, who are managing the technology portfolio of the company. The projects agreed upon are gradually transformed into utilizable products following a step-by-step transformative learning process.

The researchers have seen that, employees working at the operational level (such as production or sales) in the company mostly focus on exploitation activities and use their time for the fulfillment of their own assigned tasks rather than the generation of new ideas. When looking at the middle level management employees on the other hand; researchers realized that, the employees are explicitly asked to generate innovation by the headquarters and this causes a much greater pressure on exploration activities. In the research at the company; it has been understood that there is both contextual and structural ambidexterity, and the ambidexterity during idea formation is mostly contextual. It is also seen that exploratory activities (idea generation) are encouraged and supported by an appropriate managerial context during daily activities, and ambidexterity become structured increasingly as the ideas are strengthened and gradually transformed into R&D projects. That is to say; the people responsible with generating new ideas are specialized in appropriate organizational context (contextual) and then, a clearly defined working structure was formed for them (structural).

Also Sinha (2015), who makes studies on newly established businesses, spelled that some businesses focus more on daily events as they make an effort to understand the new activities they encounter, while some others focus too much on discovering innovations time to time, they try too much and hence cannot exploit the outputs of exploration activities in this process. For this reason he propounded that, it is not correct to express clearly how newly established companies deal with exploitation and exploration dilemma.

1.3.2 Contextual Ambidexterity

Early on, academicians have proposed different structural mechanisms for organizations to overcome among themselves competing demands faced by organizations; and organizations had implemented them. For example; some businesses took some of their employees from their current jobs for a certain period of time and set them work by forming special cross-functional teams, while others have separated different types of activities within a single business unit, and tried to run it by forming small business development teams affiliated with another business unit (Birkinshaw and Gibson 2004). However, it has been propounded that the dual structures supporting the implementation of these exploitation (beneficial) and innovative approaches separately may lead to excessive segregation, and that ambidexterity skill stems from the organizational context of a business unit. The difficulty in achieving contextual ambidexterity skill may be in getting individuals and groups to cope with the inherent tension between the processes of exploration and exploitation/benefiting (Gibson and Birkinshaw 2004). Organizational context emerges as a concept related to the alignment and adaptability of the organization, and these two capabilities refer to behavioral abilities that should simultaneously be in all business units. It is an approach that leaves the choice between alignment and adaptation oriented activities of individual employees in organizations, in the context of their daily work, to the individuals themselves. For this reason, it was stated that contextual ambidexterity is conceptualized not at the organizational level (Havermans et al. 2015), but at the individual and group level (Lavie et al. 2010). Wang and Rafiq (2014) stated that the advantages of contextual ambidexterity skill are more widely acknowledged based on the structural and temporal separation of exploration and exploitation, despite this achieving contextual ambidexterity skill involves great difficulties, and studies on this subject are still insufficient on the basis of both organizations and individuals (as cited in Havermans et al. 2015).

1.3.2.1 Alignment Ability

Gibson and Birkinshaw (2004), defined alignment as ensuring harmony between all activities in business units and directing them towards the same goals, as well as coordinating the activities in order to create value in the short term. On the other hand, they also stated that to the companies that focus too much on alignment, the short-term results they achieve will look very good, but this situation might blind companies to the extent that eventually they could not see the changes in the sector. In their study, they exemplify how the CEO of Lloyds TSB Bank Plc., headquartered in the United Kingdom, providing extraordinary shareholder returns by means of focusing on a single idea (return on equity) throughout the 1980s and 1990s. They expressed that, nevertheless, not much attention was paid to understanding the changing customer needs and workforce morale; hence, Lloyds TSB lost 60% of its market value from 1998 to 2003 (Birkinshaw and Gibson 2004).

1.3.2.2 Adaptability Ability

Gibson and Birkinshaw (2004) define adaptability as the capacity of organizations to restructure the activities in business units in order to meet changing consumer demands and to rapidly evaluate the new opportunities. They argued that, even though this skill is an important and desired one, in case companies concentrate on efforts of adaptability to the degree to sacrificing today's opportunities would mean that they will miss the occasions of the day, and build tomorrow's business. In their study, they exemplify Ericsson, which globally pioneered the mobile phone industry and developed one of the first analog mobile systems, and remarked that the impressive growth in sales achieved by Ericsson through its system business masked the high-cost and overinflated organizational structure. Adaptability activities prevailed on alignment activities. Despite the company employed 30,000 people in its R&D activities in 100 technology centers at that time, this situation caused Ericsson to be affected the most by the collapse in the telecommunications sector and the layoff of 60,000 employees (Birkinshaw and Gibson 2004).

When contextual ambidexterity and structural ambidexterity compared to each other from some aspects, the fundamental differences between them can be summarized shown as Table 1.2.

As it can be understood from Table 1.2, in structural ambidexterity; it is essential that the roles are more distinct, the chain of command is apparent and clear, and hence the employees are specialized in their jobs. It is seen that there is a mechanical organizational structure; alignment-oriented or adaptability-oriented activities should be carried out in separate units; the definition of the structure in these units, the sequence of the activities, the preference, authority and responsibility in budget allocation belong to the top management.

On the other hand, in contextual ambidexterity, there is flexibility in job descriptions; roles are not clearly defined. The important matter is to organize a structure in which employees can easily take initiative. In the performance of the tasks, the

Table 1.2 Differences between contextual ambidexterity and structural ambidexterity

	Structural ambidexterity	Contextual ambidexterity
How is ambidexterity achieved?	Alignment-focused and adaptability-focused activities are done in separate units or teams	Individual employees divide their time between alignment-focused and adaptability-focused activities
Where are decisions made about the split between alignment and adaptability?	At the top of the organization	On the front line-by sales people, plant supervisor, office worker
Role of top management	To define the structure, to make tradeoffs between alignment and adaptability	To develop the organizational context in which individuals act
Nature of roles	Relatively clearly defined	Relatively flexible
Skills of employees	More specialists	More generalist

Source Birkinshaw and Gibson (2004). Building Ambidexterity into an Organization, MIT Sloan Management Review, 45, p. 50

responsibility of allocating their time with respect to the alignment or adaptability activities assigned to them is left to the employees. It is based on the principle of completing the work with the empowerment of the staff, the learning organization structure, and the problems being handled by those who do the work without necessitating going to the top management. For this reason, those seen at the forefront are mostly the employees in positions such as salespeople, office workers, and factory managers.

1.4 Ambidexterity Management Strategies

Duncan stated in his article published in 1976, that companies should balance between efficiency and innovation and for this; they should ensure the harmony between structure and strategy. For this reason he argued that, successful companies change their structures in the course of time and gained ambidexterity successively/sequentially. Tushman and O'Reilly (1996) suggested that, the sequential application is not enough; it is more correct to carry out productivity and innovation studies simultaneously (structurally), and this can be achieved by units that are structurally separate, autonomous and aligned (harmonized) within themselves regarding human, culture, structure and process. Gibson and Birkinshaw (2004) on the other hand propounded that, in successful organizations, in order for employees to carry out activities related to productivity or innovation, they can allocate their own time to these tasks but that environments, consisting of a series of processes and systems, should be designed (contextual), so that alignment and adaptability works could be performed by the employees (O'Reilly and Tushman 2013).

When the studies on this subject reviewed; a successful development requires an action both creative and collective, and for developing a successful and perpetual product, ambidexterity is essential as Sheremata (2000) remarked. Ambidexterity makes possible both profitability and innovation in the long run (Tushman and O'Reilly 1996). It is suggested by Cameron and Quinn (1988) that, the high performing organizations try to maintain internal morale, while meeting external demands. Taylor and Greve (2006) argued that product developments that are carried out in businesses provide positive and consistent returns, while radical new products express high risk and uncertainty. Andriopolus and Lewis (2009) in their study comprising the interviews and surveys they made with successful and innovative companies revealed that, the tension of profit and exploration is paradoxical and that companies should be both profitable and creative.

Levinthal and March (1993) argued that, considering the long-term survival and success of an organization, "ensuring the current viability of the organization depends on its ability to exploitation adequately; while ensuring its future viability, its ability to make adequate exploration". Tushman and O'Reilly (1996) mentioned the existence of more than one contradictory structure, process and culture within the same company, and stated that, organizational ambidexterity is the ability to follow up both increasing and discontinuous innovation simultaneously, and that this is important for the long-term survival of companies. (O'Reilly and Tushman 2013).

Researchers have implicit or explicit knowledge processes in terms of exploitation and exploratory approaches (Floyd and Lane 2000). Researcher orientation (exploration); refers to the discovery of new products, resources, knowledge and opportunities, and is associated with experimentation, radical change, and learning. This involves the use of open knowledge bases; by internalizing and combining them supports incremental improvements that can be made for existing technological and marketing oriented works (Nonaka 1994). Exploitation, on the other hand; refers to the improvement of existing products, resources, knowledge and competencies, and is associated with incremental changes and learning, through the use and development of the enterprise's own possibilities (March 1991; Benner and Tushman 2003; Sinha 2015). Atuahene-Gima (2005) also stated that, exploitation is a process that develops and expands existing knowledge, and seeks more efficiency and improvement to ensure incremental innovation, while the exploration process requires the development of new knowledge through experimenting to encourage the diversity and innovation required by more radical innovation (Andriopoulos and Lewis 2009).

According to Lubatkin et al. (2006), ambidextrous companies can carry on simultaneous, but contradictory knowledge management processes; benefit (exploitation) from existing competencies and explore new areas of equal skill. To achieve competency organizationally, the skills possessed must be conducted well balanced. Failing that, unexploited or ignored skills will begin to become blunt. Thus, any weakness an organization may reveal will cause its competitors to get ahead of themselves, and lead to lose their competitive advantage (He and Wong 2004).

In the success of ambidexterity of the organizations, the level of analysis is vitally important, because the choices on how stresses will be solved at the level of analysis are solved at the next step in general. For example; a business unit may become ambidextrous by forming two functions or two subdivisions having different focuses. A production facility may become ambidextrous by forming two teams (one of them is responsible with elasticity developments, the other one is responsible from efficiency improvements) and a single team may become ambidexter by assigning different roles to each of the individuals (Raisch and Birkinshaw 2008).

On the other hand, depending upon the organizational culture, organizational climate and the role of the leader plays, these practices may generate synergy; as well as create problems in terms of efficiency, and implementation of strategies. At this point, in terms of gaining organizational ambidexterity, the role of the leader comes into prominence both in the formation of the favorable organizational context, and in the design of the organizational structure.

1.5 The Role of Leadership in Implementing Ambidexterity Strategies

For years, the ability of successful organizations to exist in a dynamic environment keeps its place as an important theme in organizational literature.

For maintaining their sustainable competitive advantages, enterprises must both sustain their advantageous position, and adapt to the changes that are done, as well. Businesses achieving this become effective and efficient. The businesses, having organizational ambidexterity, adapt themselves within a short period of time due to the flexibility skill they gained in the environments where uncertainty dominates, besides being effective responding to customer demands (Stubner et al. 2012; Yıldız and Karataş 2018).

When the studies on organizational ambidexterity are evaluated in general, it is stated that the premises discussed are organizational structure, behavioral contexts, leadership processes and environmental conditions (Raisch and Birkinshaw 2008). When the strategies that the organizations will determine for gaining competitive advantages and the importance of the leaders in implementation of these strategies are considered, it is thought that, the ambidexterity subject deserves many more studies to be done selecting leadership as the baseline.

Since exploration and exploitation require a different logic in principle, it is possible to say that, few companies become successful in managing ambidexterity. To implement such a strategy successfully, certain conditions and organizational characteristics are required. So much the more, it needs a special style of manager or leader (Akdoğan et al. 2009). Yet, despite the fact that the studies on ambidexterity are gaining more and more attention, and the numbers of researches are beginning to increase; it is seen that, the studies on the behavior of management staff and leaders displayed in the presence of the contradicting and conflicting demands of exploration and exploitation approaches are insufficient, and there is a need for leaders, who can balance the competing pressures and tensions of different organizational architectures (O'Reilly and Tushman 2013).

It is seen that, the studies conducted are generally related to transformational and transactional leadership behaviors. In the study made by Nemanich and Vera (2009) it has been propounded that, the transformational leadership behaviors support ambidexterity; in the study of Jansen et al. (2009) transformational leadership very much related to exploratory innovation, while the transactional leadership closely related to exploitative innovation. The results of the study conducted by Baškarada et al. (2016) on the leadership and the structure of ambidexterity based on semi-structured interview with top level managers provides support to the thesis of transformational leadership being suitable to exploratory innovation context, while transactional leadership is suitable to exploitative innovation context. It has seen that, leaders effectuate the exploitation by encouraging them through three organizational mechanisms which are training (the training process is expected to be built on the previous knowledge), performance management (providing empathy and motivation) and knowledge management (recording the new information, comparing to the old information, wide sharing instead of filtering). They have determined five leadership behaviors/qualification leaders use to effectuate exploration; commitment, vision, risk comfort, empowerment, and inclusivity. At the center of gravity of these characteristics, there are institutionalized learning, risk taking, experimenting, flexibility, and increase of diversity enforcing exploration and innovation. It has been demonstrated that creating an organization that includes the conditions under which employees can act in these behaviors can be accomplished with the skills of the leader. Contextual ambidexterity, where individuals decide when they will focus on exploitation, and when they will focus on exploration (Gibson and Birkinshaw 2004) were the mechanisms preferred to effectuate organizational ambidexterity.

Ambidexterity does not come into view from the formal structure alone or the vision statements of a charismatic leader, but rather requires the creation of a supportive context in which individuals make their own choices about how and where to focus their energies. In other words, it can be considered as a qualification, that the leadership is demonstrated by everyone in the organization. The contextual ambidexterity (Gibson and Birkinshaw 2004) in which individuals decide when to focus on exploitation and when to focus on exploration were the mechanisms preferred to promote organizational ambidexterity.

The multifaceted ambidexterity does not appear in the form of a single structure or the visionary expressions of a charismatic leader; instead needs to create a supportive bond where individuals make their own choices about how and where to focus their energies. In other words, it can be considered as a qualification that the leadership is demonstrated by everyone in the organization. The driving force oriented to ambidexterity sometimes directed by the initiatives from to downwards, but the aim herein is to allow leadership come into the view at every level of the organization (Birkinshaw and Gibson 2004).

The existence of organizational ambidexterity makes the efforts of adaptation to new market techniques, the efforts for providing differentiated product, a wide range of products and high quality products easier. That's to say, as organizational competency increases, it will be easier to carry on activities such as the optimal use of capacity, negotiating for the best price when purchasing raw materials, increasing the efficiency of production systems, and reducing production costs (Bakan and Sezer 2016).

It is known that, the top managers and the teams they formed are the responsibility centers heavily affecting the activities of organizations and playing effective roles in gaining strategic capabilities. In understanding how organizational activities arouse, the behaviors of top management teams fairly have the characteristics of reference. Within this frame, the behavioral integrity of top management teams is an important reference point in enabling to envisage the route the organizations are in. Since the principal philosophy of the organizational competency which is achieved when strategic dilemmas and conflicting activities reach a common ground, and thus ensures a balance is based on the idea of simultaneously supporting two different logics in an organization; it is to be concluded that one of the important actors involved in the construction of this idea within the organization, is the top management (Özbebek and Tunç 2017) and leading managers.

Thinking that it would not be sufficient handling ambidexterity only on company basis in the economic, social and technological circumstances of today's new world, which changes and digitalizes at an unprecedented pace, would not be wrong. There will be a need for leaders having ambidextrous (versatile) characteristics; leaders, who are able to be successful in a wider ecosystem, perceive opportunities and threats much faster, and develop appropriate strategies, while conducting exploitation and exploration activities in a balanced manner within the company. When the characteristics of the leaders are considered; there will be a need for the leaders, who are able to use their transformative and managerial skills together; besides demonstrating ethical behaviors, having political strategic skills, shortly having strategic leadership characteristics for being successful in these activities.

References

Abatecola G (2012) Organizational adaptation: an update. Int J Org Anal 20(3):274–293 q Emerald Group Publishing Limited 1934–8835. https://doi.org/10.1108/19348831211243802

Akdoğan MŞ, Akdoğan AA, Cingöz A (2009) Organizational ambidexterity an empirical examination of orgazinational factors as antecedents of organizational ambidexterity. J Glob Strat Manag 3(2):17–27. https://doi.org/10.20460/JGSM.2009318458

Anderson P, Tushman ML (1990) Technological discontinuities and dominant designs: a cyclical model of technological change. Adm Sci Q 604–633

Andriopoulos C, Lewis MW (2009) Exploitation-exploration tension and organizational ambidexterity: managing paradoxes of innovation. Org Sci 20(4):696–717. Issn 1047-7039. !eissn 1526-5455 !09 !2004 !0696. https://doi.org/10.1287/orsc.1080.0406

Atuahene-Gima K (2005) Resolving the capability–rigidity paradox in new product innovation. J Mark 69(4):61–83

Bakan İ, Sezer B (2016) Örgütsel Ustalığın Rekabet Stratejileri Üzerindeki Etkisi: Bir Alan Araştırması. Uludağ J Econ Soc /B.U.Ü. İktisadi ve İdari Bilimler Fakültesi Dergisi Cilt/ 35(2):177–203

Bakan İ, Sezer B(2017) Örgütsel Ustalığın Performans Yönetimi Üzerindeki Etkisi: Bir Alan Çalışması. KSÜ Sosyal Bilimler Dergisi. Cilt:14. Sayı:2

Barreto I (2010) Dynamic capabilities: a review of past research and an agenda for the future. J Manag 36(1):256–280
Baškarada S, Watson J, Cromarty J (2016) Leadership and organzational ambidexterity. J Manage Dev 35(6)
Benner MJ, Tushman ML (2003) Exploitation, exploration, and process management: the productivity dilemma revisited. Acad Manag Rev 28(2):238–256
Birkinshaw J, Gibson CB (2004) Building an ambidextrous organisation. Adv Inst Manage Res Paper (003)
Bodwell W, Chermark TJ (2010) Organizational ambidexterity: integrating deliberate and emergent strategy with scenario planning. Technol Forecast Soc Change 77:193–202
Brown SL, Eisenhardt KM (1997) The art of continuous change: linking complexity theory and time-paced evolution in relentlessly shifting organizations. Adm Sci Q 42:1–34
Bruns T, Stalker GM (1961) The management of innovation. Tavistock, London, pp 120–122
Burgelman RA (1991) Intraorganizational ecology of strategy making and organizational adaptation: theory and field research. Organ Sci 2(3):239–262
Burgelman RA (2002) Strategy as vector and the inertia of coevolutionary lock-in. Adm Sci Q 47(2):325–357
Cameron KS, Quinn RE (1988) Organizational paradox and transformation. In: Quinn RE, Cameron KS (eds) Paradox and transformation: toward a theory of change in organization and management. Ballinger, Cambridge, MA, pp 12–18
Cao Q, Gedajlovic E, Zhang H (2009) Unpaking organizational ambidexterity: dimensions, contingencies and synergistic effects. Org Sci 20(4):685–834 https://doi.org/10.1287/orsc.1090.0426
Caroll T (2012). Designing organizations forexploration and exploitation. J Org Des 1(2)
Cattani G (2005) Preadaptation, firm heterogeneity, and technological performance: a study on the evolution of fiber optics, 1970–1995. Organ Sci 16(6):563–580
Cattani G (2006) Technological pre-adaptation, speciation, and emergence of new technologies: how Corning invented and developed fiber optics. Ind Corp Chang 15(2):285–318
Cattani G (2008) Reply to Dew's (2007) commentary: pre-adaptation, exaptation and technology speciation: a comment on Cattani (2006). Ind Corp Chang 17(3):585–596
Chien SY, Tsai CH (2012) Dynamicc capability, knowledge, learning, and firm performance. J Org Change Manage Emerald Article 434–444
Cingöz A, Akdoğan A (2015) Örgütsel Ustalık (Organizational Ambidexterity): Örgütsel Ustalık Düzeyini Belirlemede Araştırıcı ve Yararlanıcı Stratejilerin Etkileşimsel Rolü. Aksaray Üniversitesi İktisadi Ve İdari Bilimler Fakültesi Dergisi 7(1):59–67
Colbert BA (2004) Karmaşık kaynak temelli bakış: Stratejik insan kaynakları yönetiminde teori ve pratik için çıkarımlar. Acad Manag Rev 29(3):341–358
Demirel G, Öden E, Kumkale İ (2020) Yönetim Strateji Liderlik Ed. H. Karadal, M.Halis ve G.Mert. Bölüm 6:Covit-19 Pandemisi Sonrası Sürdürülebilir Toplumlar: Toplum 5.0. s:119–136, Akademi Titiz Yayınları.İstanbul. ISBN.978-605-7604-31-6
Dew N, Sarasvathy SD (2007) Innovations, stakeholders & entrepreneurship. J Bus Ethics 74(3):267–283
Duncan BL (1976) Differential social perception and attribution of intergroup violence: testing the lower limits of stereotyping of blacks. J Pers Soc Psychol 34(4):590
Dupouet O, Tariana BC, Lakshman C (2013) Innovation from Information systems an ambidexterity approach. Springer
Floyd SW, Wooldridge B (1996) The strategic middle manager: how to create and sustain competitive advantage. Jossey-Bass Publishers
Floyd S, Lane P (2000) Strategizing throughout the organization: managing role conflict in strategic renewal. Acad Manag Rev 25:154–177
Geçkin Onat S (2017) Yakınsama Kültürü ve Online Çevresel Katılım: Greenpeace,TEMA Vakfı, Karadeniz İsyandadır Platformu Üzerinde Bir Araştırma. Global Medya Journal TR Edition 8(15) Güz/Fall

Ghemawat P, Ricart Costa JEI (1993) The organizational tension between static and dynamic efficiency. Strateg Manag J 14(S2):59–73
Gibson CB, Birkinshaw J (2004) The antecedents, consequences and mediating role of organizational ambidexterity. Acad Manage J 47(2):209–226
Gözen A (2018) Aile İşletmelerinde Aile Etkisi ve Örgütsel Ustalık Kavramlarının İşletme Performansı Üzerindeki Etkilerinin İncelenmesi. Hiperyayın:266. İstanbul. ISBN: 978-605-281-123-8. E-ISBN: 978-605-281-124-5
Grant R (1996) Toward a knowledge-based theory of the firm. Strateg Manage J 17(Winter special issue):199–122
Guiette A, Vandenbempt K (2014) Dynamics of change recipient sense making in realizing strategic flexibility: a competence-based perspective. Competence Based Manage 7:145–191. https://doi.org/10.1108/S1744-211720140000007006
Gupta A, Smith KG, Shalley C (2006) The interplay between exploration and exploitation. Acad Manage J Aug 49(4):693–706. https://doi.org/10.5465/AMJ.2006.22083026
Hammel G, Prahald CK (1993) Strategy as stretch and leverage. Harv Bus Rev 71(2):75–84
Havermans LA, Den Hartog DN, Keegan A, Uhl_Bien M (2015) Exploring the role of leadership in enabling contextual ambidexterity. Hum Resour Manage 54(S1):179–200. https://doi.org/10.1002/hrm.21764
He Z-L, Wong P-K (2004) Exploration vs exploitation: an empirical test of the ambidexterity hypothesis. Organ Sci 15(4):481–493
Hitt MA, Ireland RD (2002) The essence of strategic leadership: managing human and social capital. J Leadersh Org Stud 9(1):3. ABI/INFORM Global
Huy QN (2002) Emotional balancing of organizational continuity and radical change: the contribution of middle managers. Adm Sci Q 47(2002):31–69
Jansen JJP, Tempelaar MP, van den Bosch FAJ, Volberda HW (2009) Structural differentiation and ambidexterity: the mediating role of integration mechanisms. Org Sci 20(4):797–811
Kauppila OP (2010) Creating ambidexterity by integrating and balancing structurally seperate interorganizational partnerships. Strateg Org 8(4):283–312. https://doi.org/10.1177/1476127010387409
Kets de Vries MFR (1995) Life and death in executive fast lane. Jossey Bass, San Francisco
Kumkale İ (2016) Organization's tool for creating competitive advantage: strategic agility. Balkan near Eastern J Soc Sci 02(03):118–124
Lavie D, Stettner U, Tushman ML (2010) Exploration and exploitation within and across organizations. Acad Manage Annals 4(1):109–155
Levinthal D, March J (1993) Myopia of learning. Strateg Manag J 14:95–112
Lubatkin MH, Şimşek Z, Ling Y, Veiga JF (2006) Ambidexterity and Performance in small-to medium-sized firms: the pivotal role of top management team behavioral integration. J Manage 2006 32:646. https://doi.org/10.1177/0149206306290712
Luecke R (2008) Managing creativity and innovation. İş Dünyasında Yenilik ve Yaratıcılık.Çev.Turan Parlak.Türkiye İş Bankası Kültür Yayınları.İstanbul
March JG (1991) Exploration and exploitation in organizational learning. Organ Sci 2(1):71–87
Mom TJM, van den Bosch FAJ, Volberda HW (2007) Investigating managers' exploration and exploitation activities: the influence of top-down, bottom-up, and horizontal knowledge inflows. J Manage Stud 44(6):910–931
Nelson A, Harvey FA (1995) Technologies for training and supporting your agile workforce. In: Creating the agile organization: models, metrics and pilots, proceedings 4th agility forum annual conference, Bethlehem, PA
Nemanich LA, Vera D (2009) Transformational leadership and ambidexterity in the context of an acquisition. Leadersh Q 20(1):19–33
Nonaka L (1994) A dynamic theory of organizational knowledge creation. Organ Sci 5:714–737
O'Reilly CA, Tushman ML (2013) Organizational ambidexterity: past, present and future. Acad Manage Perspect 27(4):324–338. https://doi.org/10.5465/amp.2013.0025

Özbebek Tunç A (2017) Örgütsel Çift Yönlülük. İşletmelerde Denge Arayışında Üst Yönetimin Rolü. Beta Basım A.Ş.ISBN. 978-605-333-852-9.İstanbul
Peters TJ (2001) Leadership: sad facts and silver lining. Harv Bus Rev 79(11):121–128
Quinn RE, Cameron K (1983) Organizational life cycles and shifting criteria of effectiveness: some preliminary evidence. Manage Sci 29(1):33–51
Raisch S, Birkinshaw J (2008) Organizational ambidexterity: antecedents, outcomes, and moderators. J Manage 34(3):375–409. https://doi.org/10.1177/0149206308316058. http://jom.sagepub.com/cgi/content/refs/34/3/375
Raza A, Murad HS (2014) Learning new management viewpoints: recontextualizing strategic leadership in global and regional context. Bus Rev 9(1)
Sanchez R, Mahoney JT (1996) Modularity, flexibility, and knowledge management in product and organization design. Strateg Manag J 17(S2):63–76
Sastry MA (1997) Sıçramalı bir örgütsel değişim modelindeki sorunlar ve paradokslar. Adm Sci Q, 237–275
Senge PM (1990) The fifth discipline the art and practice of the learning organization. ISBN 0-385-26095-4. Copyright ©1990 by Peter M. Senge. Published By Doubleday
Sheremata WA (2000) Centrifugal and centripetal forces in radical new product development under time pressure. Acad Manage Rev 25(2):389–408
Shrivastava P (1986) Postmerger integration. J Bus Strateg. https://www.emerald.com/insight/content/doi/10.1108/eb039143/full/pdf?title=postmerger-integration
Sinha S (2015) The exploration-exploitation dilemma: a review in the context of managing growth of new ventures. Vikalpa. J Decis Makers 40(3). https://doi.org/10.1177/0256090915599709
Smith ME, Prieto IM (2008) Dynamic capabilities and knowledge management: an integrative role for learning? Br J Manag 19:235–249. https://doi.org/10.1111/j.1467-8551.2007.00543.x
Smith WK, Tushman ML (2005) Managing strategic contradictions: a top management model for managing innovation streams. Organ Sci 16:522–536
Spender J-C, Kessler EH (1995) Managing the uncertainties of innovation: extending Thompson (1967). Hum Relat 48(1):35. ABI/INFORM Complete
Stubner S, Blarr WH, Brands C, Wulf T (2012) Organizational ambidexterity and family firm performance. J Small Bus Entrepreneurship 25(2):217–229
Tan J, Wang L (2010) Flexibility–efficiency tradeoff and performance implications among Chinese SOEs. J Bus Res 63:356–362
Taylor A, Greve HR (2006) Superman or the fantastic four? Knowledge combination and experience in innovative teams. Acad Manage J 49:723–740
Tushman ML, Anderson P (1986) Technological discontinuities and organizational environments. Adm Sci Q, 439–465
Tushman ML, Romanelli E (1985) Organizational evolution: a metamorphosis model of convergence and reorientation. Res Org Behav
Tushman ML, O'Reilly CA (1996) Ambidextrous organizations: managing evolutionary and revolutionary change. Calif Manage Rev 38:8–30
Wang CL, Rafiq M (2014) Ambidextrous organizational culture, contextual ambidexterity and new product innovation: a comparative study of UK and Chinese high-tech Firms. Br J Manag 25(1):58–76
Yıldız H, Karataş G (2018) Kuzeydoğu Anadolu Bölgesi'ndeki KOBİ'lerde Örgütsel Ustalık (Çift Yönlülük):Çatışan Stratejilerin Birleşimi. Manisa Celal Bayar Üniversitesi Sosyal Bilimler Dergisi. Cilt:16, Sayı:4

Chapter 2
Strategic Leadership

Abstract Since today's businesses generally try to survive by struggling in the red oceans, they have to make decisions (with incomplete information) in an environment of constant uncertainty or in conditions that lose their certainty in a very short period of time. For this reason, the classical and traditional managerial characteristics of business managers are not sufficient for the management of businesses operating in such environments. The long and the short of the matter, there is a need for leader managers who have the appropriate behavior and management skills in all conditions, who are capable of solving problems in an environment dominated by complexity and chaos, creative, strategic thinker, in a visionary structure that can adapt his enterprise to change and transformation, open to cooperation, communication and negotiations, supporting doing the right thing, using ethics as base, supervising when necessary to get the job done right. Leaders having these skills, which we can express as strategic leadership skills, are more and more important for organizations. When the studies on this subject and the theories that contribute to the literature are reviewed, although the basic points are similar, it is seen that there are different perspectives and different models are put forward. It is thought that each of the models discussed in this section will provide benefits to businesses in different ways and can be used in practices according to needs.

Keywords Strategic leadership · Managerial · Transformational · Political · Ethical · Communicative

2.1 Introduction

The era, we are in, is defined by experts as variable (V), uncertain (U), complex (C) and ambiguous (A), due to the fact that it is an era, where the speed and scope of change cannot be determined, predictions are not done, and long-term plans cannot be made (Bayraktar 2018). As the pace of social, economic and technological change accelerates; wherever they are and whatever the type of activity they carry on, organizations must take increasingly complex decisions in the face of an uncertain future (McKinsey & Company 2019). This situation has started to compel organizations as well to ensure their sustainability on national and international basis by keeping

İ. Kumkale, *Organizational Mastery*, Accounting, Finance, Sustainability, Governance & Fraud: Theory and Application, https://doi.org/10.1007/978-981-16-7582-9_2

in step with the changes they are in. The unprecedented speed of developments in communication technologies and mobility has increased the dimension of competition, making it compulsory for leaders to follow new and different strategies in order to cope with issues such as better examination of the internal and external environment, perception of problems, and evaluation of opportunities (Güllüce et al. 2019). While foresight and determination of long-term strategies were important until recently, now it became important the ability of changing agility of strategy and besides bringing employees rapidly in the ability of adaptation and acting towards the new goals. Here it is seen that, in this VUCA era to stay strong requires more flexibility and endurance than ever before (Bayraktar 2018). Therefore, the value of those who have the ability to solve complex problems, think creatively and strategically tend to increase (McKinsey & Company 2019).

When they are evaluated with respect to strategic management, it is understood that the strategic leadership skills make the organizations much more successful than others (Hitt and Ireland 2002). The reason of this is that strategic leadership is an understanding that focuses on the characteristics and behaviors of managers and leaders who know what is experienced both in the internal and external environment and how to act against these events besides who have strategic management awareness (Güllüce et al. 2019). Strategic leadership; refers to the ability to make consequential decisions (as well as wisdom) about ends (goals), paths (strategies) and means (actions) in uncertain environments (Pisapia 2006). On the other hand, according to Baterman and Snell (2016), the strategic leader is the person who foresees a livable future for the organization and puts the idea of creating this future together with employees and initiating the change. When the concept of strategic leadership used by John Adair in the 1980s is examined, it is seen that the strategic leader is the person who achieves in the fullest extent of the whole what many leaders have to achieve for certain jobs or departments, and in fact, among the leadership styles it is the leadership style that includes the characteristics that every leader should have. Since the strategic leaders are the people who create a vision, shape strategic changes by foreseeing the future, provide competitive advantage and have the ability to make effective decisions in complex environments (Narkiyotik 2020), they have a leadership structure that is suitable for today's complex and uncertain conditions.

According to Gulliot (2003), strategic leadership grounds on organizational values, standards and ethics. Then knowledge, expertise, continuous training and development come. Taking responsibility, authorization (and delegation) and accountability follows this development process. At this point commitment deepens and motivation increases. Taking advanced training to develop strategic thinking skills increases the competence of individuals, and this creates an opportunity to use their strategic competence to support a strategic leader in every situation. Eventually, the individual participates in the strategic decision-making process and becomes a strategic leader (Fig. 2.1).

When the body of literature is examined, it is seen that the concepts are nest together in the studies under the titles of strategic leader, strategic leadership, strategic leadership models and strategic leadership styles. At the same time, though strategic

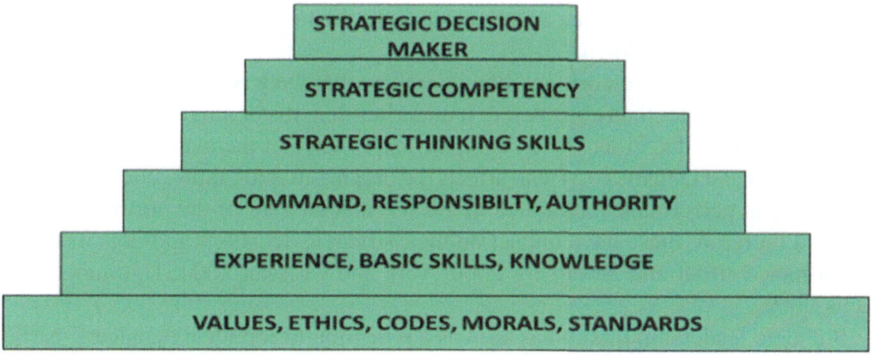

Fig. 2.1 Strategic Leadership Pyram. *Source* Guillot (2003) https://www.semanticscholar.org/paper/1-Strategic-Leadership-%3A-Defining-the-Challenge-Guillot/5e2555b4f0805c8fd1401625b65cb6ede12a6938. Accessed on 17.04.2021

leadership is included in modern leadership approached in some studies, in many others it is included in post-modern (contemporary) leadership approaches.

When looking at the comprehensive leadership studies, the change in the content over time is noticed. It is seen that the studies were based on the great men school and trait theory in the early twentieth century (who propounded that leaders should have certain characteristics), continued with behavioral leadership theory (focused on human and work-oriented behavior) in the 1950s and 1960s, and after the 1960s, taking into account the contingency theories (it is argued that there are different leadership styles suitable for every situation). Albeit these theories known as classical (traditional) leadership theories have important contributions to the subject of leadership, due to autocratic leadership, democratic leadership and bureaucratic leadership styles in this period cannot fully answer the questions about leadership, modern leadership approaches have been suggested. These approaches examined the various aspects of leadership processes that are not previously considered very often. The approaches such as transformational leadership, transactionalist leadership, charismatic leadership, instructional leadership, political leadership were expressed among modern approaches; later on lots of leadership approaches such as visionary leadership, strategic leadership, entrepreneurial leadership, innovative leadership etc. were discussed as contemporary approaches (Yılmaz 2020).

During 1960s and 1970s, when basic causes of the state of affairs and circumstances organizations encountered have been considered as managerial behaviors and organizational outputs, and even though actually believed that leadership is not a concept that would affect the organization performance too much (Ireland and Hitt 2005), in 1980s this opinion has begun to change (Akyüz 2018). The "Upper Echelon Theory", the roots of which have been founded with *"Environment, Strategy, and Power within Top Management Teams"* named article published in 1981 by Hambrick (Özbebek Tunç 2017) and have been proposed by the study titled *"Upper Echelons: The Organization as a Reflection of Its Top Managers" published in 1984 by*

Hambrick and Mason, became an important factor in this change (Davies and Davies 2004; Akgemci 2008; Akyüz 2018).

On the basis of this theory involving the view that leadership skills on organizations are much larger than considered; it underlies that, the demographic characteristics such as age, educational level, company experience of the manager (Daily et al. 2002; Bakan and Doğan 2013) who affects the organizational outputs such as strategy and financial performance, redound up the sort and amount of the information they use, and therefore these have impact on their strategic decisions and organizational performance (Boal and Hooijberg 2000; Vera and Crossan 2004; Uğurluoğlu and Çelik 2009).

Strategic leadership theory has seen as a reflection of top level managers, particularly the CEOs (Chief Executive Officer). Numerous CEOs undertake the responsibilities of strategic leadership off their own bat. However, the unpredictability of the environmental conditions in the organizations by the globalization in which the twenty-first century brought within the organizations, and the new competitive structure of the global economy has required to benefit from the individuals who are responsible in creating the future of the business instead of only an individual's point of view (Ireland and Hitt 2005). Yet, the view of primary responsibility in effective strategic leadership should be under the top management, particulary under the CEO would be appropriate is common (Uğurluoğlu and Çelik 2009).

2.2 Strategic Leadership Models

In this section, strategic leadership models prominent in literature studies (Kumkale and Çetin 2016; Naktiyotik 2020); John Adair's "The Three Circle Model", Davies and Davies' "Nine Point" strategic leadership model, the "Three Dimensional" strategic leadership model of Ülgen and Mirze(2018) addressing the issue by pointing out "Hard Factors and Soft Factors" and Pisapia's "Five Dimensional" strategic leadership model will be covered.

2.2.1 John Adair's "The Three Circles Model"

John Adair (2013), argued that the characteristic distinguishing the strategic leadership from other leaderships is in conferring the responsibilities on the whole, not on the departments, and explained his views with a three-circles model. He stated that the model is suitable for both teams and organizations, and these characteristics consist of three general functions that can be expressed in a simple way: 1. Motivating and developing the individual, 2. Organizing and maintaining a team, 3. Achieving the common goal (Fig. 2.2).

Adair (2013) thinks that, when the general role of strategic leadership indicated in three circles is divided it creates seven functions. He lists these as (not in order of

Fig. 2.2 Broad functions of strategic leadership. *Source* Adair (2013). *Effective strategic leadership*. Translation: Salih Fatih Güneş. 3rd Printing. Babıali Kültür Yayıncılığı, Istanbul. ISBN: 975-8486-20-9

importance); to determine a direction for the whole of the organization, to follow a successful strategy and policy, to ensure the execution (comprehensive administrative responsibility), to organize and reorganize (balance between the whole and its parts), to reveal the spirit of the institution, to connect the organization to other organizations and to the whole society, selecting the leaders of today and raising the leaders of tomorrow.

2.2.2 "Nine-Point Strategic Leadership Model" of Davies and Davies

Davies and Davies (2010) stated that it is not always easy to distinguish between the characteristics of "effective, good leadership" and "strategic leadership" in studies, and pointed out that strategic leaders have three basic characteristics: 1. Strategic leaders are strategic thinkers, 2. Strategic leaders are strategic learners, 3. Strategic leaders focus on values.

Davies and Davies (2004), in their nine-point strategic leadership model have discussed five organizational abilities and four individual characteristics and underlined that in strategic leadership both individual characteristics and organizational abilities should exist together (Fig. 2.3.)

They propounded organizational abilities as; strategic focusing, transforming strategy into action, aligning individuals and organizations, determining effective strategic intervention points, developing strategic skills, and the individual abilities as; not being content with what is available, attaching importance to strategic thinking and learning, creating a cognitive model for their own understanding and practices, and having personal and professional networks.

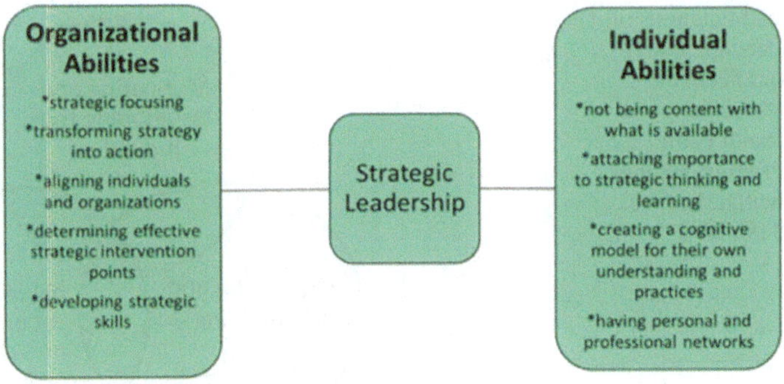

Source Davies and Davies (2004)

Fig. 2.3 Davies and Davies's strategic leadership model. *Source* Davies and Davies (2004)

2.2.3 The Strategic Leadership Model of Ülgen and Mirze Addressing the "Hard and Soft Factors"

Ülgen and Mirze (2018) stated that strategic analysis and strategy selection are the elements requiring a rational and objective perspective by means of analytical analyses and hence they are defined as the hard factors in the literature. On the other hand, they propounded that the strategic management process is not only composed of hard factors, but also this work has a human aspect and since the people who make and implement the strategies are people having different values, ideas and characteristics, so the issues related to human are described as soft factors (Fig. 2.4). They emphasized that, because of this above mentioned reason, in the studies on strategic leadership, the soft factors related to human should be considered. In the strategic

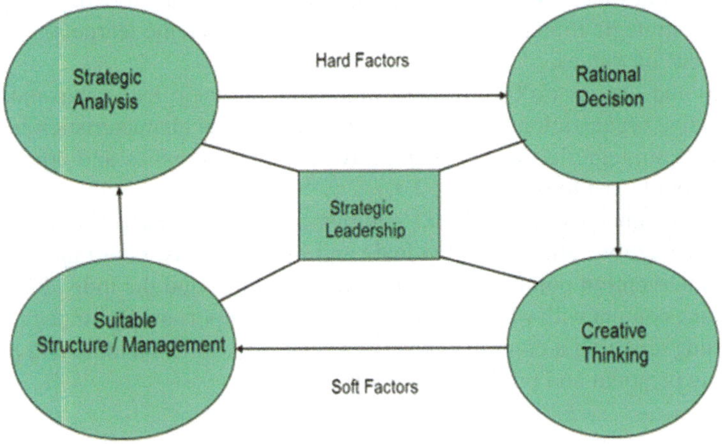

Fig. 2.4 The strategic leadership model of Ülgen and Mirze. *Source* Naktiyotik (2020)

leadership model of the authors there are three leadership styles: Operational (traditional) strategic leadership, visionary strategic leadership, transformational strategic leadership.

2.2.4 *Five Dimensional Strategic Leadership Model of Pisapia*

Pisapia (2006) argued that leaders should carry on business in a multifaceted reality and hence this creates a need for a versatile series of leadership actions. He stated that in the new era we are in, the old leadership models are not sufficient, conditions require models to be revised, and this post-modern era demands leaders who maximize the agility and adaptability of organizations. According to Pisapia strategic leadership requires managing, transforming, bonding, bridging and bartering leadership actions, it is important to be able to use these behavioral patterns when and where necessary and in the fastest way (behavioral agility). At the same time, strategic leadership is a powerful model that combines leadership with management, politics with ethics, strategic intent with tactics and actions, and builds a bridge between the old and the new. For this reason, strategic leadership characteristics are the most suitable leadership type for the conditions of our age (Pisapia 2009).

Pisapia, in his work named "*The Strategic Leader: New Tactics for a Globalizing World*" (2009), expressed the actions required by strategic leadership as follows;

Managing: Taking the necessary actions to achieve the predetermined objectives and goals effectively and effectively.

Transforming: Changing organizational conditions and organizational culture, enabling the change by influencing employees' ideas and actions.

Bonding: To establish trust in the organization, to make it unique not only among individuals but to the whole system, on the other hand, to create emotional attachment to the values and aspirations of individuals.

Bridging: To establish and enhance the necessary connections to develop alliances with people who have power and influence, both inside and outside the organization, in order to obtain the resources and support needed to carry out the work.

Bartering: Being open to negotiations in order to meet the needs of individuals and the goals of the organization, to strengthen the relations and alliances, working with a win–win principle.

Pisapia asserted that these five actions are multiple leadership actions specific to strategic leaders and stated that these actions will bring behavioral agility to leaders if they are used according to the situation they are in.

In the research, the strategic leadership dimensions based on the strategic leadership model developed by Pisapia will be included in details since it contains many opinions propounded by the studies in the literature.

2.3 Dimensions of Strategic Leadership

Leaders know their organizations well. They well know all the characteristics of both the individuals and groups that make up the organization, and thus, they can move the organization from where it is to where they are targeted. Yet, while it was easier to do this in the past, it has become quite difficult today. Because in the past, many things seem more loud and clear, today it is getting more and more ambiguous (Pisapia 2009). The first quarter of the twenty-first century was therefore the years when significant strategic leadership skills were needed. In leadership vision is very important and it starts with a dream. That dream can become a vision only when you start working for that dream. However, the formation of the vision is needless to say not enough for an organization and a strategy is required. It requires a very important and integrated skill to determine the conditions right and realistic that the organization is in, to create a correct and logical vision and to act quickly for this vision, to actualize the transformation when necessary, to convince the audience and make them cooperate.

Strategic leadership is organized around four key tensions that leaders face at all levels and in every aspect of life. These tensions are between "what can be" and "what is", and between "what is right" and "what is possible" (Pisapia 2006).

2.3.1 *Managerial Strategic Leadership*

Leaders in Managerial Leadership understanding take roles to use resources in the most efficient way, manage organizational activities in the most effective way (Yeşilyurt 2007) and affect only the actions and decisions of the people they work together with (Rowe 2005). They endeavor to create an effective communication environment that will contribute positively to the motivation of the employees, to establish balance by considering the organization as a whole, to create a positive perception by representing the organization within the internal and external environment. They always try to find the most effective way to get the contributions of the audience at the highest level (Uğurluoğlu and Çelik 2009). The effectiveness of the managerial leader increases to the extent it meets the personal needs of the employees (Eroğlu and Akkoç 2012). They have more expertise in functional areas, they are better at managing short-term goals. Therefore, they appear to be involved in situations and contexts in daily activities (Hambrick 1989). Although it is stated that managerial leaders are not very good at creating value for their organizations, it can be said that they are quite good at preserving and maintaining the created values (Rowe 2001; Eren 2011). Apparent and explicit situations in which the circumstances do not vary widely and require the application of predetermined principles are appropriate contexts to work for them. It is a type of leadership that performs management activities through actions in the form of planning, organizing, directing and controlling, and is generally more stable and does not tend towards changes unless it is necessary. For this type of leaders, to act in accordance with the chain of command and to apply rules, policies and procedures is important.

A managerial leader is a problem solver, even if he/she directs his energy to reach the goals, to use resources efficiently, to maintain the organizational structure stable or canalize the people to work in this direction. In solving problems he/she seeks the best ways so that people can continue to contribute to the organization and at the same time make them achieve the necessary results. Being a managerial leader requires not genius or heroism, but perseverance, determination, hard work, intelligence, analytical ability, tolerance and goodwill. According to the managerial leader, goals arise from necessities and are therefore profoundly rooted in the history and culture of the organization. Managerial leaders tend to see working as a facilitating process. They assist the process by calculating opposing interests, planning when controversial issues should rise, and lowering tensions.

On the one hand they negotiate and bargain; on the other hand they resort to rewards (conditional rewarding), penalties (management with exceptions) and other forms of pressure (Uğurluoğlu and Çelik 2009). According to them, everyone has to take responsibility for their work.

2.3.2 Transformational Strategic Leadership

Transformational leaders set the orientation for their organizations. They have a range of skills that can effectively initiate transformation (Keçecioğlu 2004). According to Akdemir (2018), large scale transformations depend on not being obsessive and being able to abandon the established thoughts for transformation. Therefore, in transformational leadership; the ability to be creative, brave, set a vision, draw direction, work with a team and form competent teams, and a positive perspective are required. At the same time, there is a need to be knowledgeable in many subjects and to have in-depth knowledge on a few subjects. Bass (1990) described transformational leadership with seven characteristics: charisma, inspiration, mental stimulation, individual level attention, conditional reward, management with exceptions, and emancipatory leadership (Keçecioğlu 1998; Çetin 2020), Hambrick (2007) stated that the transformational leadership approach put forward by Bass is actually a by-product of the strategic leadership approach.

In transformational leadership, it is important to motivate employees by taking into account their individual differences, to create awareness about the vision and mission, and to encourage employees to look beyond their own interests for overall improvement. The leader can achieve this in many ways. Being *charismatic* in the eyes of its followers is the center of success. He/she gives excitement them by inspiring that they can do great things with a little extra effort. He/she creates energy by providing intellectual stimulation and shows the new and different ways of looking at old problems to employees. They act as mentors to those who need help, can meet their emotional needs (Bass 1990). The transformational leader realizes the existing tendencies, needs and desires of his audience or potential audience and uses them to motivate the audience (cited by Karip 1998).

Transformational leaders are an important pioneer who on one side strives to build the collective trust and strength needed for groups to succeed while dealing with challenges (Bass et al. 2003). They initiate reforms and innovations in creativity and innovation oriented organizations and influence employees by changing mission, vision, strategy, activities and functions (Ceylan et al. 2005). Transformational leadership style is more effective than other leadership styles in environmental contexts characterized by uncertainty, change, and stress (Bass et al. 2003). Therefore, Latham (2013) argued that although systems and forces are needed for change and transformation, they are inert and lifeless without leaders. On the other hand, the connection of transformational leadership with values also puts emphasize on how much important the role of values in strategic leadership (Carter and Greer 2013).

2.3.3 Political Strategic Leadership

It is a type of leadership that focuses on increasing and maintaining power, allocating resources where necessary to facilitate organizational success and using them effectively. Maintaining the status quo is important to support individuals and organizational goals in this type of leadership (Pisapia 2006). For this reason, they exhibit behaviors aimed at expanding their sphere of influence and developing mutual relationships. Political leaders view their followers as rivals and take care to develop relationships with them by negotiating and meeting their needs. They are utilitarian (exploitative) and try to do everything possible to satisfy as many people as possible. They do not leave the aids and supports they received unpaid. Achieving the goals is important for them, so they use actions such as promising rewards, developing partnerships, negotiating, and building relationships. They behave eagerly to negotiate for getting things done. They support reconciliation and find a reconciliatory common ground in differences of opinion. They maintain their relationships with a wide range of people, for performing their work and solve problems they reach out to people who are effective when they see it necessary. In resolving conflicts, they try to find solutions that will benefit (win–win) both sides. When necessary, they develop partnerships with people or institutions outside the organization. This ability, which is based on developing interdependent relationships, constitutes the balancing part of leadership (Pisapia 2009).

2.3.4 Ethical Strategic Leadership

Ethical leadership was defined by Brown et al. (2005) *as demonstrating normative appropriate behavior through personal actions and interpersonal relationships, and introducing such behaviors to followers through two-way communication, empowerment and decision-making*. According to the researchers, the behaviors of ethical leaders, such as honesty, trustworthiness, fairness, and diligence, that they exhibit and are normatively appropriate by their followers, make the leader a legitimate and reliable role model. By behaving so, it is possible for them to use rewards and punishments to encourage ethical behavior and make decisions based on ethical values. While these combine the hallmarks of ethical leadership, none of these aspects alone cover all of the requirements of ethical leadership.

The ethical leader reveals behaviors that are deemed appropriate to be supported and encouraged in the organization, as well as behaviors that are not deemed appropriate and should be avoided (Akşit 2020). It is important for leaders to make the right ethical choices while performing their roles in the organization (Bakan and Doğan 2013). With their ethical awareness, honest character, and accountability (Brown et al. 2005), they strive for the universally right things, work for the benefit of the organization and others, and stand against unethical behavior.

The ethical leader should be able to act proactively in the face of events, have the ability to make the right decisions, and the decisions they made should be correct, fair and accurate. A leader, who is believed to make ethically correct decisions and is trusted, contributes significantly to the development of such ethical-based behaviors and social values within the organization. This situation plays a role also in increasing organizational commitment (Bakan and Doğan 2013) and the work performance (Yukl et al. 2011) of the units.

In fact, carrying on an ethical or responsible business is to ensure that the leader improves the moral compass and the organization has a reliable compass as well. Ethical leadership uses this moral compass to guide personal actions and the company. The important thing is to create the ethical atmosphere in the organization. This is all about shaping the organizational culture and climate. Since no leader can do this alone, they need the support of their senior staff, but ultimately, but eventually the responsibility and direction of this belongs to the leader (Leigh 2013).

2.3.5 Communicative Strategic Leadership

Leading is based on communication. Communication is like the nervous system of leadership (T.B.B. 2017). The ability to lead others is largely based on the individual's ability to communicate, which is influenced by the context in which he or she is. In different contexts different results may occur. In other words, leadership that is effective in one context may not be effective in another. For this reason, communicative leaders who have creative and improvised communication skills with correct observation under all conditions can make their positioning correctly without hiding behind systems (Hamrefors 2010).

Communication is of great importance for a leader both in the organization and in their activities outside the organization. For example, sharing information, conducting meeting, giving instructions, correction, explanation, planning, strategy setting, negotiation, etc. many situations require correct and good communication (T.B.B. 2017).

In communicative leadership, facilitative communication is at stake. Therefore, besides the importance of listening, it is more important to really hear what is being said and to integrate with the main subject, to have the ability to move the conversation further (www.timepr.com). Communicative leaders are leaders who are in dialogue with the audience, give active feedback and expect this from others, implement participatory decision-making processes and are perceived as the person involving. They coach, enable the staff to manage themselves (self-management), create structures that facilitate work. They are responsive, respectful and approachable to their staff. They put forward their expectations clearly and unambivalently, demonstrate this in terms of quality, productivity and professionalism. If it is desired to develop the communicative leadership skills of both the individual managers and the management team in an organization, the organization should adapt these characteristics to its context and culture (tbb.gov.tr).

Communicative leaders support governance; listens to the ideas and opinions of the employees, takes and evaluates what they see suitable to the need. Interaction occurs with communication, and the opportunity for governance arises with interaction. Thus, leaders give employees the opportunity to participate in management, that is, to have a say in management.

Organizations never operate in isolation. They are always in contact with their external environment. In addition, communicative leaders communicate and develop close relationships with influential people outside the organization who they think might have an impact on getting things done. Their communication networks are strong. At the same time, it is easier to exit the negotiations with the right and desired benefit when necessary by means of the communication skills of such leaders. Creating a good communication process is also closely related to having the ability to empathize.

References

Adair J (2013) Effective strategic leadership. Çeviri: Salih Fatih Güneş. 3. Baskı. Babıali Kültür Yayıncılığı, İstanbul. ISBN: 975-8486-20-9

Akdemir A (2018) Liderlik ve Vizyon Yönetimi. İstanbul. Beta Basım Yayım Dağıtım.A.Ş.

Akgemci T (2008) Stratejik Yönetim. Ankara. Gazi Kitabevi. ISBN: 978-9944-165-17-4

Akşit H (2020) Etik Liderlik. In: Uysal HT, Aksoy C, Yılmaz F (eds) Liderlik Tarzları: Çağdaş Yönetim Yaklaşımıyla İnsan Sanatında Ustalaşma içinde. Nobel Akademik Yayıncılık, Ankara, s.303–314

Akyüz M (2018) Stratejik Liderlik. Stratejik Yönetim Araştırmaları Dergisi. Cilt:1. Sayı 1:45–66

Bakan İ, Doğan İF (2013) Liderlik.Güncel Konular ve Yaklaşımlar.Ankara. Gazi Kitabevi. ISBN. 978-605-344-071-0

Bass BM (1990) From transactional to transformational leadership: learning to share the vision. https://discoverthought.com/Leadership/References_files/Bass%20leadership%201990.pdf. Accessed on 16 Apr 2021

Bass BM, Avolio BJ, Jung DI, Berson Y (2003) Predicting unit performance by assessing transformational and transactional leadership. J Appl Psychol 88(2):207

Bateman TS, Snell SA (2016) Management/Yönetim. Çeviri Editörleri: Senem Besler & Cihat Erbil, Ankara. Nobel Yayıncılık

Bayraktar N (2018) Stratejik Çeviklik ve Çevik Liderlik. Kaynak.Baltaş Grubu. *İnsan ve Değişim.* Sayı: 75. http://www.kaynakdergisi.net/makaleler.asp?sayi=75&sira=991. Accessed on 17 Jan 2021

Boal KB, ve Hooijberg R (2000) Strategic leadership research: moving on. Leadersh Q 11(4):515–549

Brown ME, Trevino LK, Harrison DA (2005) Ethical leadership: a social learning perspective for construct development and testing. Hum Decis Processes 97(2):117–134. https://doi.org/10.1016/j.obhdp.2005.03.002

Carter SM, Greer CR (2013) Strategic leadership: values, styles, and organizational performance. J Leadersh Org Stud 20(4):375–393

Ceylan A, Keskin H, Eren Ş (2005) Dönüşümcü ve Etkileşimci Liderlik ile Örgütsel Bağlılık Arasındaki İlişkilere Yönelik Bir Araştırma, İstanbul Üniversitesi İşletme Fakültesi Yönetim Dergisi, Yıl:16. Sayı 51:33

Çetin OI (2020) Dönüşümcü Liderlik. In: Uysal HT, Aksoy C, Yılmaz F (eds) Liderlik Tarzları: Çağdaş Yönetim Yaklaşımıyla İnsan Sanatında Ustalaşma içinde. Nobel Akademik Yayıncılık, Ankara, s. 83–98

Daily CM, Mc Dougall PP, Covin JG, Dalton DR (2002) Governance and strategic leadership in entepreneurial firms. J Manage 28(3):387–412

Davies BJ, Davies B (2004) Strategic leadership. School Leadersh Manage 24(1):29–38. https://doi.org/10.1080/1363243042000172804

Davies B, Davies BJ (2010) The nature and dimensions of strategic leadership. ISEA 38(1):5. https://pdfs.semanticscholar.org/d69f/9b41da930b9b0dd42a2a6cd7d888e6cae11b.pdf. Accessed on 14 Mar 2021

Eren E (2011) Yönetim ve Organizasyon: Çağdaş ve Küresel Yaklaşımlar.10. Baskı İstanbul. Beta Basım Yayım Dağıtım AŞ. ISBN: 978-605-377-506-5

Eroğlu A, Akkoç İ (2012) Liderlikte Güncel Yaklaşımlar Editörler: Akif Tabak, Harun Şeşen, Tolga Türköz. Ankara. Detay Yayıncılık. ISBN: 978-605-5216-17-7

Guillot WM (2003) Strategic leadership: defining the challenge. Air Space Power J. Maxwell AFB 17(4):67–75. (Winter 2003)

Güllüce AÇ, Kaygın E, Zengin Y, Sağbaş MV, Karabal C (2019) Stratejik liderlik anlayışının örgütsel özdeşleşme ve işten ayrılma niyeti ile ilişkisi: İstanbul ili örneği. Uluslararası Akademik Yönetim Bilimleri Dergisi. Cilt 5(7):30–47

Hambrick DC (1989) Guest editor's introduction: putting top managers back in the strategy picture. Strateg Manage J 10:5–15. Special Issue: Strategic Leaders and Leadership

Hambrick DC (2007) Editor's forum upper echelons theory: an update. Acad Manage Rev 32(2):334–343

Hamrefors S (2010) Communicative leadership: modern leadership in value-creating networks. http://hamrefors.se/Publikationer/Communicative_Leadership.pdf. Accessed on Apr 18 2021

Hitt MA, ve İrlanda RD (2002) Stratejik Liderliğin Özü: İnsan ve Sosyal Sermayeyi Yönetmek. Liderlik ve Örgütsel Çalışmalar Dergisi 9:3–14. https://doi.org/10.1177/107179190200900101

Ireland RD, Hitt MA (2005) Achieving and maintaining strategic competitiveness in the 21st. century: the role of strategic leadership. Acad Manag Exec 19(4):63–74

Keçecioğlu T (1998) Liderlik ve Liderler. KalDer Yayınları. No: 24. İstanbul, Mavi tanıtım ve Pazarlama Ltd. Şti. ISBN: 975-6851-007

Keçecioğlu T (2004) Stratejik İnsan Kaynakları Yönetimi. İstanbul, Sistem Yayıncılık

Kumkale I, Çetin OI (2016) Stratejik Liderlik. Liderlik Üzerine Yazılar. Ed.A. Sinan Ünsar, içinde Bölüm III. Paradigma Akademi.İstanbul, s: 85–107. ISBN: 978-605-66861-7-7

Latham JR (2013) A framework for leading the transformation to performance excellence part I: CEO perspectives on forces, facilitators, and strategic leadership systems. QMJ vol 20, No. 2/ASQ

Leigh A (2013) Ethical leadership: creating and sustaining an ethical business culture. Great Britain and United States. Kogan Page Limited

McKinsey&Company (2019). Want better strategies? Become a bulletproof problem solver. https://www.mckinsey.com/~/media/McKinsey/Business%20Functions/Strategy%20and%20Corporate%20Finance/Our%20Insights/Want%20better%20strategies%20Become%20a%20bulletproof%20problem%20solver/PDF-Want-better-strategies-Become-a-bulletproof-problem-solver.pdf?shouldIndex=false. Accessed on 6 Jan 2021

Naktiyotik S (2020) Stratejik Liderlik. In: Uysal HT, Aksoy C, ve Yılmaz F (eds) Liderlik Tarzları:Çağdaş Yönetim Yaklaşımıyla İnsan Sanatında Ustalaşma içinde. Nobel Akademik Yayıncılık, Ankara, s.165–176

Özbebek Tunç A (2017) Örgütsel Çift Yönlülük. İşletmelerde Denge Arayışında Üst Yönetimin Rolü. Beta Basım A.Ş. ISBN. 978-605-333-852-9. İstanbul

Pisapia JR (2006) Mastering change in a globalizing world: new directions in leadership. ISBN-13: 978-962-8077-00-7, ISBN-10: 962-8077-00-7. Faculty of Education Hong Kong Institute of Educational Research. The Chinese University of Hong Kong

Pisapia JR (2009) The strategic leader: new tactics for a globalizing world. ISBN 978-1-60752-152-5(pbk). ISBN 978-1-60752-153-2(hardcover). IAP-Information Age Publishing. Inc. USA

Rowe WG (2001) Creating wealth in organizations: the role of strategic leadership. Acad Manage Executive 15(1):81–94. https://www.academia.edu/26317027/Creating_wealth_in_organizations_The_role_of_strategic_leadership

Rowe WG (2005) Creating wealth in organizations: the role of strategic leadership. Acad Manag Exec 15(1):81–94

Time public relations. Stratejik Lider İletişimi. https://www.timepr.com/stratejik-lider-iletisimi/. Accessed on Apr 18 2021

T.B.B. (Türkiye Belediyeler Birliği) (2017) İletişimsel Liderlik ve Gelişimsel Yönetim. https://tbb.gov.tr/online/kitaplar/iletisimsel_liderlik_ve_kentsel_gelisim_2017/html5forpc.html?page=18&bbv=1&pcode=. Accessed on Apr 18 2021

Uğurluoğlu Ö, Çelik Y (2009) Örgütlerde Stratejik Liderlik ve Özellikleri. *Hacettepe Sağlık İdaresi Dergisi.* Cilt: 12. Sayı:2

Ülgen H, Mirze SK (2018) İşletmelere Stratejik Yönetim. Güncellenmiş 9. Baskı. Beta Basım Yayım Dağıtım A.Ş. ISBN: 978-605-242-270-0. İstanbul

Vera D, Crossan M (2004) Strategic leadership and organizational learning. Acad Manag Rev 29(2):222–240

Yeşilyurt E (2007) Akademik ve Yönetimsel Liderlik. Doğu Anadolu Bölgesi Araştırmaları Dergisi 5(3):76–80

Yılmaz F (2020) Liderlikle İlgili Temel Teoriler. In: Uysal HT, Aksoy C, ve Yılmaz F (eds), Liderlik Tarzları: Çağdaş Yönetim Yaklaşımıyla İnsan Sanatında Ustalaşma. İçinde. Nobel Akademik Yayıncılık, Ankara, s.17–40

Yukl G, Mahsud R, Hassan S, Prussia GE (2011) An improved measure of ethical leadership. J Leadersh Org Stud 20(I):38–48. https://doi.org/10.1177/1548051811429352. https://www.researchgate.net/publication/258152783

Chapter 3
Organizational Agility

Abstract In the first quarter of the twenty-first century we are in; global business trends and tackling environmental turbulence are pushing businesses more and more. From past to present, various factors such as natural disasters, epidemics, environmental and political problems affecting the world, as well as global economic crises, have affected organizations in some way during or at the end of the process. Besides many businesses affected negatively, it is seen that there are also organizations having strategic agility that emerge from the process by gaining strength. In order to talk about the strategic agility of organizations; their *competencies* in organization, human resources, technology resources, planning, etc. (ability to meet goals and intentions), their *flexibility* (its adaptability to changing market and environmental conditions with its resources), their *responsiveness* (being sensitive to recognizing changes, perceiving opportunities and threats, being able to meet changing customer demands) and to be able to use these abilities as quickly as possible (*quickness*) are all important. The crisis created by the Covid-19 Pandemic, which is still being fought, can also be seen as an opportunity for organizations to re-evaluate themselves in order to understand how speed and to what extent they can adapt to new conditions, and in a sense, their agility. Hence, an omnibus study conducted in 2021 showed that skill development efforts and closing skills gaps in the workforce for the companies became a high priority. Regardless of what the businesses live today and will experience in the future, it would be right to ensure they are strategically resilient against the unknown and to work on dynamic planning processes to rise to the top.

Keywords Agility · Organizational agility · Competency · Responsiveness · Quickness

3.1 Introduction

It is stated that, in this period where we live the first quarter of the twenty-first Century, most of the companies have difficulties in dealing with global business trends and environmental turbulence, their financial and non-financial performances have rapidly decreased due to the insufficient understanding of strategic agility and its dimensions (Arokodare and Asikhia 2020); moreover, the number of companies

İ. Kumkale, *Organizational Mastery*, Accounting, Finance, Sustainability, Governance & Fraud: Theory and Application, https://doi.org/10.1007/978-981-16-7582-9_3

named as "Zombie" Companies all around the world is gradually increasing. Bank for International Settlements/BIS, in its "Zombie Companies: Their Anatomy and Life Cycle" titled report, published in September 2020, mentioned about the Zombie companies as "smaller, much more inefficient, more indebted, and the companies less investing in physical and intangible capital." In the report it was remarked that, these companies also perform poorly for years before they turned into zombies, and over time 25% of those zombie companies disappeared from the market, and 60% of them quit zombie status. It has been evaluated that these zombie companies, which seem to have improved, continue to perform poorly compared to healthy companies, and that they are more likely to become zombie companies again, according to healthy companies. Another issue particularly emphasized by BIS is that, more zombie companies will exist in the process of exit from the Covid-19 Pandemic, and this situation will bring slower and inefficient recovery (Bulkan 2020). Pandemic, the economic crisis brought about by this pandemic or search of the situation of the zombie companies are not within the scope of our study. However, organizations' adaptation to sudden and/or rapidly changing conditions, not only in crisis periods, but also them being prepared for new conditions they may encounter at any time, and creating new and realistic strategies depend on their strategic agility. For example, it is seen that the US-based Amazon share prices rose due to the increase in online sales, and according to the Bloomberg Billionaires Index, Jeff Bezos has strengthened his place as the world's richest person (with a fortune of $ 136 billion). This situation can also be attributed to the fact that e-commerce is an advantageous sector due to the general rise during the pandemic period. However, the description in the report of the American Bank JP Morgan about the subject is not to be overlooked: "Amazon is not only the most profitable company, but it is also a company, which has the best operational opportunities, and is most well positioned one for such a period" (https://www.bbc.com/turkce/haberler-dunya-52303413). In this context, the concept of strategic agility (Khoshnood and Nematizade 2017), which is a dynamic capability, will be explained in detail.

3.2 Conceptual Framework

Firstly, the concept of agility will be explained, then the concepts of strategic agility and organizational agility will be discussed, and the theoretical infrastructure will be formed by giving information about the characteristics of organizational agility.

3.2.1 Agility

In today's world where technological developments in production, consumption, market and communication are experienced very rapidly, it is important for organizations to have the ability to develop and when needed to change their structures, operations and activities at the same speed in order to adapt to this development and change. Perceiving the change rapidly, taking measures and implementing them quickly means to respond quickly to change; that is to be agile (Kumkale 2016). Agility comes from the Latin word "agilitas" and means the ability to think quickly and draw conclusions easily, as well as being physically quick and active (Latdict Latin Dictionary & Grammer Resources 2019). The concept of agility was first used in "*twenty-first Century Manufacturing Enterprise Strategy Report*" published in 1991. In the report prepared with the aim of finding solutions to the problems of the decline and loss of competitiveness in the US manufacturing industry; which in the project led by Roger Nagel, Operations Director of Lehigh University, Iacocca Institute, the concept of "agile production" as a new production system emerging in industrialized countries has been comprehensively discussed. In the report it was suggested that agile manufacturing technology can be a powerful competitive weapon with a non-technical vision and synthesis of management and social values (Nagel 1992). Agile manufacturing is defined as the ability to survive and being sustainable by developing in a competitive environment where a continuous and unpredictable fluctuation exist and also the customers design products and services and direct the markets according to their wishes and demands (Gunasekaran 1999). The concept of agile production systems is also stated by Raj et al. (2012) as an expression, which involves speed, alertness, ability, flexibility-, systematic approach, social sensitivity, economy, environmental awareness, innovation, and excellence. Jin-Hai et al. (2003) stated in their study that there are five elements in the nature of a real agile production and listed them as (1) strategic processing, (2) multiple-winners, (3) integration, (4) core competence, and (5) information technology. According to them, agile production is in fact a competitive work, but it is provided by cooperation. Although agility was initially developed on production strategies aimed at increasing the competitiveness of companies with the concept of agile production, it has become a concept, a perspective, and a management approach that deals with the entire organization, and over time with the help of expressions of strategic agility and organizational agility, it became associated with strategic management.

3.2.2 Strategic Agility

While creating a long-term defensible position was sufficient for companies to gain competitive advantage in the past; in order to sustain day by day increasing competition it has emerged the need to be managed with strategies that can adapt to changing conditions, that is, the strategies must be agile (Eisenhardt and Brown 1998). Some authors stated that strategic agility is the speed, flexibility and ability of organizations to reduce turbulent business hazards and defined this (strategic agility) as an important determinant of organizational success (Ayub et al. 2014). Strategic agility is defined as an organization's ability to forecast and detect changes in its operating environment through the opportunities and threats it faces, and to take action and proactively respond quickly by recombining the resources, processes and strategies. In other words, strategic agility is an organization's ability to quickly adjust its choice strategy in the face of uncertainty/uncertainties (Khoshnood and Nematizade 2017; Nkuda 2017). According to another definition created by Arokodare and Asikhia (2020), inspired by different studies, strategic agility is to show that it can be successful in a competitive environment through sensitivity, competence, flexibility, and speed capabilities in order to gain competitive advantage in the market. When the different definitions in the literature are reviewed, the common concepts related to strategic agility, it is seen that the common concepts related to strategic agility are speed, flexibility, and gaining competitive advantage by having quick response skills. Of course, in order to have these skills and use these skills in practice, there are some issues that need to be dwelled on throughout the organization, including structure and process.

In order to talk about the strategic agility of organizations, organization, human resources, technology resources and planning issues are important. Since, strategic agility involves predicting future events and preparing for them in a systematic and realistic way, planning is also an issue that should not be ignored in this process (Oyedijo 2012). It should also be expressed that, strategic agility is an enterprise-wide capability that includes a holistic understanding involving many processes, such as organizational structures, information systems, logistics processes besides the structure, and in short mindsets (Araza and Aslan 2016). Yusuf et al. (1999) also stated that agility includes four main concepts that are increasingly gain acceptance, and these concepts are *core talent management, creating virtual organizations, the ability to reshape, and knowledge-based enterprise*. According to Jin-Hai et al. (2003), expressed core competencies as very important and key in agility, and defined core competency as collective learning that focuses on developing and coordinating different skills and abilities. They likened these differences in skills and abilities to the hidden roots of a tree, arguing that together they increase their strength and that they should be used to create basic products to be utilized in various business operations. They are of the opinion that the core talent at the highest level in the hierarchy is the best use of all resources and abilities and exceeds the boundaries of enterprises. At this point, it is possible to talk about the benefit of creating virtual organization structures. This is because companies participating in the virtual organization benefit from more than their own assets. In other words, the organization will increase its competitive advantage due to the wider organizational scope of the virtual organization. On the other hand, this wide organizational scope can also cause integration problems. For crossing the boundaries of the organization/enterprise, integrating the core competencies requires organizational learning, intense relationship, involvement and commitment. It seems useful to address the basic elements of knowledge and learning at this point.

Elements of knowledge, learning and core competence Jin-Hai et al. (2003) (Fig. 3.1):

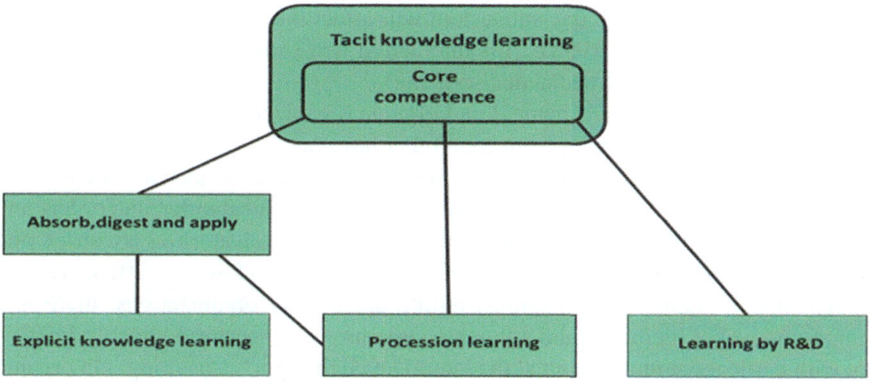

Fig. 3.1 Relationship between learning and core competence. *Source* Jin-Hai et al. (2003)

- The learning of explicit knowledge is the ability to obtain knowledge from external sources, but accessing knowledge in this way is not an institutional core competence. However, if knowledge is captured, imbibed, internalized and used in the organization's practice in its area of expertise, it can be a core capability of the business to a certain extend and represent a potential core competence.
- Work learning, also referred to as process learning, is "learning by doing". During the process of a job, all kinds of transactions and activities performed allow to gain many experiences and information. This is of great importance for an organization as it broadens the scope of knowledge and core competence.
- Learning through R&D can be considered as the most important form of learning. Because it is not possible for innovation to develop without R&D, and at the same time, innovation is the basis and source of sustainable advantage.
- Tacit knowledge refers to the knowledge in minds, that is, non-coded, non-formal knowledge, and can be shared experientially and transferred by mutual learning. This form of learning can provide connectivity to core competence and expand the scope of the core competencies. In order to become explicit knowledge, tacit knowledge should be put on the record. However, this requires the sharing of information in a reliable environment and the integration of information.

3.2.3 Organizational Characteristics of Agile Organization

Considering that organizations as an open system are in constant interaction with their environment, it is important for an agile organization to have some organizational characteristics in order to respond quickly to changing internal and external environmental conditions. Organizations are not only in a dynamic environment consisting of many systems larger or smaller than themselves, but also a whole consisting of many sub-systems that interact dynamically with each other. Since subsystems are interdependent, changes in one subsystem will affect the behavior of other subsystems and the whole (Alıç 1995). This interaction will show differences in different organizational structures (mechanical-organic).

Thus, the concepts of mechanical and organic organization have been formed in literature and their differences from each other have been revealed.

Mechanical organizations are the structures where clearly defined hierarchy gains importance, expert roles are distributed within this hierarchical order, and orders and instructions flow from top to bottom. Job descriptions are clear, rules are strict, and everyone is expected to follow procedures and protocols (Jewczyn 2010). On the other hand, in organic organizations, unlike mechanical organizations, there is a minimum level of hierarchy and a flexible structure. They perform the coordination not with vertical commands, but at the lateral level, through "consulting". In organic organizations, the ideas of employees are taken into account; this in turn paves the way for teamwork and strengthens existing teams. They have functional expertise and the knowledge received from outside is valuable to organic organizations. In an organic organization, there are no rigid job descriptions; instead there is a strong central communication network (Sine et al. 2006). There is a shared set of values and goals rather than managed behavior, instructions, and rules. Downward communication from senior executives has the characteristics of advisory rather than instruction (Jewczyn 2010).

Considering the mechanical organization and organic organization structures; It is claimed that the studies showing that bureaucratic structure and thus formality are ineffective and unsuccessful in coping with innovation and change are more than the studies with positive effects (Kılıç et al. 2012). While mechanical organizations are seen as suitable for more static environments, organic structures are seen as the structures suitable for more dynamic environments.

In Table 3.1, the characteristics of agile organizations and their organizational characteristics are discussed. When the table is examined in terms of authority, rules and procedures, coordination, structure and human resources practices, it is seen that the features are compatible with the organic organizational structure. With a horizontal structuring with less hierarchy, less rules and procedures, connections between functions are emphasized and teamwork is preferred with loose boundaries. Although top management has an important function in determining direction, the hierarchy in agile organizations is not a hierarchy of authority, but a hierarchy of competence. The organization operates with an interactive communication dynamic, both horizontally and vertically (Denning 2016). Employees are strengthened through technical and ambidexterity training and human resources management practices such as workforce development, rotation, and job enrichment.

Autonomy in decision-making is ensured by facilitating access to information and knowledge, expanding authorization related to the task and empowering personnel, and coordination is carried out in an informal way.

The role of human resources, which is the most important resource for an organization, is very important in the creation of agile organizations. In other words, if the human resource of an organization is not agile, then it is not possible to mention about the agility of that organization. Because being agile is not only being able to

Table 3.1 Organizational features of agile enterprises

Organization	Features
Authority	Decentralized knowledge and control Fewer power differentials (fewer titles, levels, status dimensions, etc.) Less adherence to authority and control Loyalty and commitment to project or group Authority tied to tasks Authority change when tasks change Wide span of control rule
Rules and procedures	Few rules and procedures Low level of formal regulation (in respect to job description, work schedules) Fluid role definitions Informally organized
Coordination	Informal and personal coordination Delegation of tasks and decision making Network communication Goal-directed
Structure	Flat, horizontal, matrix, networked or virtual structure Teamwork, cross-functional linkages Loose boundaries among function and units
Human resource management applications	Employee empowerment Employee involvement Job rotation Job enrichment Autonomy in decision making Information and knowledge access Teamwork Multifunctional teams Multiple skills trainings Workforce development and training Differentiation and diversity development

Source Sherehiy et al. (2007)

anticipate change and adapting to it, but also to create the conditions yourself as an organization by noticing the change that may occur in the future and taking action in a proactive way. For this, there is a need for a workforce that can both create the structure, adapt to the newly created structure, change, new ideas and technology by displaying a positive attitude, take measures by sensing the problems that change will create, and provide solutions by taking initiative when necessary. Uncertainty and change always create stress. A flexible and resilient workforce that can cope with stress, namely that can be tolerant to unexpected situations is one of the fundamental skills of an organization (Table 3.2). To put it briefly, having an agile workforce and making this competence sustainable are the most important factors that will bring competitive advantage.

Table 3.2 Characteristics of agile workforce

Agile workforce	
Proactive	Anticipation of problems related to change Solution of change related problems Personal initiative
Capacity to adapt	Interpersonal and cultural adaptability Spontaneous collaboration Learning new tasks and responsibilities Professional flexibility
Flexibility and resilience	Positive attitude to changes, to new ideas, technology Tolerance to uncertain and unexpected situation Coping with stress

Source Sherehiy et al. (2007)

3.3 Dimensions of Organizational Agility

When the literature is reviewed, it is understood that many studies have been carried out on organizational agility and models have been put forward. At the same time, it is seen that the most striking common dimensions in the studies are competence, flexibility, and ability to respond quickly and speed. For this reason, these dimensions are explained below in order to form a basis for the four-dimensional scale developed by Sharifi and Zhang (1999), which we used in our field research.

3.3.1 Competency

Competence refers to the ability of organizations to meet their goals and intentions (Sharifi and Zhang 1999). From a resource-based perspective; companies should try to align their resources with customer needs while creating a strategy to fulfill their long-term and/or short-term goals and objectives. If the resources at their disposal are not sufficient or appropriate to fulfill these objectives, they should endeavor to perform the changes and transformation by creating new resources (in-house or creating a collaborative environment outside the company, if necessary, improving if there is an existing cooperation). These efforts are directly related to the capabilities of the organization. The ability of organizations to put into good use of the tangible or intangible resources they have with the skills they have shown the competence of that organization. The more competencies an organization has, the more likely it will be to gain competitive advantage. The resources of the company refers to the company's tangible assets such as its properties, equipment, patents, production and information technologies, and distribution systems as well as refers to its intangible resources such as the company's well-known and trusted brand name, organizational culture, knowledgeable and creative workforce, a good management team, competent human resources such as a visionary leader, and an appropriate organizational structure. Producing low cost and high quality goods and services by making maximum use of the possibilities bring in competence (ability to actualize). The transformation of a resource into competence with skills and then into competitive advantage depends on features such as unavailability, non-replicability (size of scale-, physical difference, unknown reasons for success), length of time, non-substitutable (Akdemir and Konakay 2012).

3.3.2 Flexibility

Flexibility refers to adaptability, which is the ability to meet various goals using the equipment and facilities available to the business (Sharifi and Zhang 1999). It is the ability of organizations to trigger different processes by taking into account their strengths and weaknesses in the face of changing conditions and to act reactively or proactively, through internal and external environmental analyzes that they constantly carry out, and thus to use the opportunities they have in the most efficient way in new conditions. Companies may sometimes need to produce different types and models of products (goods/services) and sometimes produce different quantities of products, depending on the need in the market. It is important that the company can be flexible enough to change its behavior according to these needs. Similarly, making revisions to adapt the human resources policies to the current conditions is important for the flexibility of the company. Establishing a learning organizational culture enables the company to better understand the behavior of customers, competitors and market regulators and to obtain better information about them. Knowledge-intensive organizations that recognize the importance of knowledge sharing are always creative and versatile (ambidexter) in solving problems. Therefore, the increase in organizational learning within the company, thanks to flexible working conditions and empowered employees, lays the groundwork for strategic agility (Uğurlu et al. 2019).

Flexibility is an important weapon in the survival of organizations today and is a measure that minimizes the negative effects and reflections of any crisis that may be encountered (Keçecioğlu and Çiçek 2015).

3.3.3 Responsiveness

Being responsive for recognizing changes means the ability to take advantage of changes by thinking quickly (Sharifi and Zhang 1999). Every passing day, changes occur in demand and purchasing behavior of customers, and this makes it necessary to respond quickly to changes (Keçecioğlu and Çiçek 2015). Responding quickly requires strategic responsiveness, insight and foresight. Strategic responsiveness refers to the firm's ability to understand the changes occurring in its environment and to perceive the opportunities and threats it may face in the future (Clauss et al. 2021). Having insight (awareness of one's own strengths and competencies) is a highly beneficial skill for the company to differentiate itself from its competitors by creating added value for customers. Foresight, on the other hand, is the ability to see facts that cannot be seen clearly and unblurred before competitors, and to understand beforehand how an affair will be in the future.

Sampath et al. (2021) believe that, strategic responsiveness is linked to many of the abilities of an organization, and also, and requires many actions such as delving the market, foresight, analysis and synthesis, that real insight can be obtained by learning from customers and competitors, and by closely examining the industries in which it operates, as well as the industries it is connected with, keeping itself up-to-date with the trends and latest developments. Thus, having information about customers' expectations, competitors' activities and cost structures will enable them to respond to change in the fastest way and get the most out of changing market opportunities for organizations.

Responding is not always linked to strategies directly related to the products themselves. Changing social value judgments, expectations of stakeholders, environmental developments, increasing sensitivity on these issues (supporting activities to prevent global warming, measuring ecological footprint, protecting bio-capacity, preventing air, water, soil pollution, etc.), government policies, and a reactive or proactive attitude to be taken in the face of changes in global trade conditions are also indicators of responsiveness. It is possible to express that, the more and wide spread the proactive behavioral models are, the more a business's ability to respond quickly is advanced.

For ensuring organizational strategic agility, which is an important element of creating competitive advantage and being sustainable, it is understood that responding to different conditions, whether environmental or technological, is directly proportional to the increase in people's competencies (Keçecioğlu and Çiçek 2015).

3.3.4 Quickness

It refers to the ability to accomplish goals, objectives and tasks in the shortest possible period of time (Sharifi and Zhang 1999). For agile organizations, the agile teams are the unanimous topic of almost everyone. It is thought that, small productive teams have greater quickness and performance to get things done. However, it is not easy to form high-performance, self-organizing teams, and having such teams and human resources should be considered as one of the basic competencies for organizations (Denning 2016). By means of today's developing information technologies and the increase in mobility possibilities (information, people, product and finance), it is much easier for everyone to reach all kinds of resources than in the past. In fact, it can be said that the only factor that reveals the difference between competitors is the willing and fast work of human resources. The speed of the company in production processes, in introduction of new products to the market, in distribution of goods and services and in their timely delivery to the customers is important in creating competitive advantage. In terms of quickness, employees' (internal customer) commitment to their organization and organizational goals, their trust in their leader, and their motivation are also important factors in the differentiation of businesses with their competitors. On the other hand internal customer satisfaction will positively affect the external customer (industrial and/or end users) satisfaction.

3.4 The Effects of Agility in Creating Competitive Advantage

The globalization of production and consumption, rapid and devastating technological change and anomaly (*irregulation, normlessness*) have brought competition to the highest levels. It is not easy to say that for an organization to have a single strategy that applies to all its competitors is sufficient in a world where temporary advantages exist. It is possible to think that the more competitors a company has, the more strategy it has (D'Aveni et al. 2010).

Strategic agility provides the opportunity to be flexible, adapt and respond quickly to changes, and implement actions to control uncertainty and risk in the market to the organizations (Sherehiy et al. 2007). In fact, agile organizations tend to seize potential opportunities in a turbulent environment by thinking beyond adapting to change. They acquire a niche with their competencies and innovations (Armstrong 2000; Chamanifard et al. 2015). In having strategic agility, it is important for the managers of the organization to constantly monitor the internal and external environment and to act proactively by using the information they have obtained. On the other hand, it will be beneficial to implement human resources strategies that will contribute significantly to the strategic agility practices of organizations and to provide the required skills and talent profile (Ahammad et al. 2020). Eventually, regardless of the position, the role and importance of human resources in the process of making strategic decisions and their implementations cannot be denied. A good leader, a good team, a good organizational climate and culture are the basic competencies that can create a competitive advantage and that cannot be imitated, copied or substituted.

Burns and Stalker (1961) argued that in a dynamic environment where environmental changes are too much, formalizing organizational form increases the risk of failure of the organization by reducing organizational adaptation to this dynamism of the environment.

On the other hand, they defined the organic structure which they stated as the ideal in forming an organization as a structure where "*the tasks are not divided into specializations, they are carried out by providing role flexibility without firmly defining the tasks and authorities connected to each functional role*" (Sine et al. 2006). A couple of experimental studies carried on related to mature organizations have supported the inverse relationship between formalization and company performance in dynamic environments (Sine et al. 2006).

Some authors stated that while it is reasonable to make recommendations for incumbent companies with rigid and formal bureaucracies to be more flexible and adaptable in dynamic environments, the same recommendations may not be appropriate for new ventures. Because it is thought that not formalizing the roles in the organizations at the beginning stage may lead to role ambiguity (Sine et al. 2006).

Every business wants to gain a competitive advantage, turn this advantage into a competitive superiority and make this superiority sustainable too. Yet, as it is not always possible to create blue oceans and competition generally takes place in red oceans, it is not easy to achieve a sustainable competitive superiority. Therefore, many resources, factors, and skills must be engaged simultaneously, in synchronization.

In order to gain sustainable competitive advantage for businesses, their tangible and/or intangible resources must have four characteristics. These are; the resources should be valuable, rare, inimitable and non-substitutable (Bal 2010).

The century we live in has quite advanced possibilities in terms of communication technologies. When this is evaluated from the perspectives of the producer and the consumer, it creates both advantages and disadvantages for both of them. From the consumer's point of view; although it is possible for the consumer to access all kinds of information about goods and/or services globally, there is also a risk of being exposed to information pollution. From the point of view of manufacturers or vendors; in addition to the possibility to learn the expectations of the consumer more quickly and to follow their competitors more easily, the fact that all businesses use this information to stand out causes the competition to accelerate and harden day by day. If we keep the border neighbors apart, even though the borders of the countries are far from each other, in fact, all businesses in the world are in competition with each other. Information and communication technologies remove these borders. Opportunities and threats arise for every business at the same time, but whichever businesses are more agile in the market, those businesses benefit from the opportunities, those businesses perceive the threats first and take their precautions. In this way, they are either not affected by the crises and manage the crises, or they get over with the least damage and continue on their way.

Albeit times and reasons change, it is always possible to encounter changes, transformations and crises, and living with crises is becoming more and more habitual. Regardless of their causes and sizes, crises affect all organizations at certain levels. The last crisis created by the recent Covid-19 Pandemic, which we are currently in, has also been a measurement test in terms of showing how quickly and to what extent organizations can adapt to new conditions. While some businesses had to end their activities with great difficulty, some chose the path of tackling difficulties, while others increased their resilience and competitiveness. It is seen that organizations that became successful and strengthened in this process have the ability to adapt quickly and easily to new and suddenly developing conditions, find suitable exit ways (strategy) and turn the crisis into an opportunity.

In the markets full of uncertainties and environments where opportunities and threats are constantly in flux, companies become successful to the extent that their managers and organizational structures respond to these changing conditions. Companies that are the leaders in their sectors have achieved this success not with superior market conditions and resources, but with their strategic agility and vigilance. With these qualities, they were able to grasp properly the opportunities that their competitors were late to notice and take advantage of, survived in the crises that destroyed the smaller ones, and some even came out of these crises stronger (Capital 2006).

According to the results of the survey Diedrich et al. (2021) conducted with senior executives, in which they measured the competitiveness of the companies of the Covid-19 crisis; propounded that, while 42% of the respondents said that the crisis weakened the competitiveness of their businesses, 28% said that it increased their competitiveness on the average. Those who stated that they were successful claimed that their companies responded quickly, handled the crisis very effectively and performed this through business model innovation.

The trend in the new business model was found to be in five areas: (1) New digital experiences, products and services in response to changes in customer behavior and needs, (2) New partnerships within and outside the industry, (3) Supply chain and operating model arrangements, (3) Supply chain and operating model regulations (arrangements), (4) Sales model changes, (5) Product development through faster iteration. As it was seen, businesses that can adapt themselves to changing conditions such as the increase in electronic commerce due to the pandemic, by means of renewing or developing business models to improve their digital infrastructure in this direction, making changes in their supply chain and sales models, and gravitate towards the products suitable for changing needs, that is, the businesses that act agile have been successful.

According to the results of a global survey conducted by McKinsey (2021), representing all regions, industries, company sizes, functional specialties and tenures, it was found that companies place more emphasis on skills development efforts than before the Covid-19 pandemic. According to this study, facing a global crisis such as the Covid-19 pandemic abruptly affecting the whole world has shown that closing skills gaps in the workforce has become a high priority in organizations. The research has shown that skill development is more prevalent than pre-pandemic, and 69% of organizations are doing more skill building than they did before the Covid-19 crisis, also these efforts focused on 'social', 'emotional' and 'advanced cognitive' skills (leadership, critical thinking, decision-making, project management). Despite the fact that, basic digital skills have also a clear priority over pre-pandemic, they are less common in developed sectors and industrial establishments (possibly due to their pre-pandemic existence).

As it can be understood from the explanations, for an organization neither adopting only the Resource-Based View (RBV) Theory, nor implementing only the Industrial Organization Theory (I/O) considering the effects of the external environment will be sufficient in competition and in fact, It is seen that the hybrid RBIO Theory

(**R**esource-**B**ased and **I**ndustrial **O**rganization Theory), which is formed by the integration of the strong points of both theories is important in achieving sustainable competitive advantage (Nkuda 2017). It is also important for leaders to have this perspective in developing organizational skills to create strategically agile organizations. Because, whatever the current and future events bring to the businesses, it is necessary to work on dynamic planning processes to ensure that they are strategically resilient and to reach the top. For this, it is clearly seen that, it is necessary to work to become companies that are flexible, fast, and able to respond instantly and increase their basic competencies.

References

Ahammad MF, Glaister KW, Gomes E (2020) Strategic agility and human resource management. Hum Resour Manage Rev 30(1). https://doi.org/10.1016/j.hrmr.2019.100700

Akdemir A, Konakay G (2012) Stratejik Yönetim. Editörler:Ali Akdemir&İ.Cemil Ulukan. Anadolu Üniversitesi. Eskişehir. ISBN 978-975-06-1349-4

Alıç M (1995) Örgütler. Eğitim Yönetimi, Yıl:1, Sayı:1, Kış 1995. https://dergipark.org.tr/tr/download/article-file/108740. Accessed on 5 May 2021

Araza A, Aslan G (2016) Yönetimde Paradigmalar, Kurumsal Çeviklik ve İmprovizasyon, Bobel Yayınları, Ankara

Armstrong M (2000) The name has changed but has the game remained the same? Empl Relat 22(6):576–593

Arokodare MA, Asikhia OU (2020) Strategic agility: achieving superior organizational performance through strategic foresight. Global J Manage Bus Res Adm Manage 20(3). Version 1.0 Year 2020. Online ISSN: 2249-4588 & Print ISSN: 0975-5853

Ayub A, Arzu F, Iftekhar H, Hafeez S (2014) Entrepreneurial call for strategic agility in fast-paced business environment. Acta Universitatis Danubıus. 10(3):2014

Bal Y (2010) Rekabet Avantajı Yaratmada Kaynak Temelli Yaklaşım Bağlamında İnsan Kaynaklarının Rolü. https://dergipark.org.tr/en/download/article-file/289118. Accessed on 29 Apr 2021

Bulkan D (2020) Pandeminin örttüğü global tehlike: Zombi şirketler. Z raporu. https://www.zraporu.com/analiz/pandeminin-orttugu-global-tehlike-zombi-sirketler/. Accessed on May 01 2021

Capital (2006) Stratejik Çeviklik Tartışması. https://www.capital.com.tr/capital-dergi/capitalde-bu-ay/stratejik-ceviklik-tartismasi. Accessed on Sept 28 2016

Chamanifard R, Nikpour A, Chamanifard S, Nobarieidihe S (2015) Impact of organizational agility dimensions on employee's organizational commitment in foreign exchange offices of Tejarat Bank, Iran. Euro Online J Nat Soc Sci 4(1):199–207. Special Issue on New Dimensions in Economics, Accounting and Management ISSN 1805-3602. http://www.european-science.com

Clauss T, Abebe M, Tangpong C, Hock M (2021) Strategic agility, business model innovation, and firm performance: an empirical investigation. IEEE Trans Eng Manage 68(3):767–784. https://doi.org/10.1109/TEM.2019.2910381

D'aveni RA, Dagnino GB, Smith KG (2010) The age of temporary advantage. Strateg Manage J 31:1371–1385. Wiley. https://doi.org/10.1002/smj.897

Denning S (2016) Understanding the three laws of Agile. Strateg Leadersh 44(6). ISSN: 1087-8572

Diedrich D, Nortcote N, Röder T, Sidor S (2021) Strategic resilience during the COVID-19 crisis. Strateg Corporate Finance Pract. https://www.mckinsey.com/business-functions/strategy-and-corporate-finance/our-insights/strategic-resilience-during-the-covid-19-crisis. Accessed on 5 Mar 2021

Eisenhardt KM, Brown SL (1998) Competing on the edge: strategy as structured chaos. Long Range Plann 31(5):786–789. Cited by Salih, A.A. and Alnaji, L. (2014). Impact of strategic thinking and strategic agility on strategic performance: a case study of Jordanian insurance industry companies. Int Rev Manage Bus Res 3(4). ISSN: 2306-9007

Gunasekaran A (1999) Agile manufacturing: a framework for research and development. Int J Product Econ 62(1–2):87–105. https://doi.org/10.1016/S0925-5273(98)00222-9

Jewczyn N (2010) Assessing mechanistic and organic organizational structures: measuring organizational uncertainty and determining an organization's proper structure. J Bus Manage Entrepreneurship 1(6)

Jin-Hai L, Anderson AR, Harrison RT (2003) The evolution of agile manufacturing. Bus Process Manage J 9(2):170 – 189. Permanent link to this document: https://doi.org/10.1108/14637150310468380

Keçecioğlu T, Çicek A (2015) Örgüt DNA' sına Yerleşen Yeni Bir Kavram ve Marka: Örgütsel ve Stratejik Çeviklik (Örgütsel Bağışıklık Sistemini Güçlendirmek). Marmara Üniversitesi İktisadi ve İdari Bilimler Dergisi 33(2):295–308. Retrieved from https://dergipark.org.tr/tr/pub/muiibd/issue/499/4515

Khoshnood NT, Nematizade S (2017) Strategic agility and its impact on the competitive capabilities in Iranian private banks. Int J Bus Manage 12(2):220. https://doi.org/10.5539/ijbm.v12n2p220

Kılıç A, Sakarya F, Erün T (2012) Örgütsel Biçimsellik ve Yenilikçilik: Kamu ve Teknopark Firma Çalışanları Üzerine Bir Araştırma. In: 1st International Interdisciplinary Social Inquiry Conference. https://www.academia.edu/1846403/%C3%B6rg%C3%BCtsel_bi%C3%A7imsellik_ve_yenilik%C3%A7ilik

Koronavirüs salgınıyla hangi şirketler yükselişe geçiyor (2020) https://www.bbc.com/turkce/haberler-dunya-52303413 Accessed on 01 May 2021

Kumkale I (2016) Organization's tool for creating competitive advantage: strategic agility. Balkan Near Eastern J Soc Sci 02(03)

Latdict Latin Dictionary & Grammar Resources (2019) https://latindictionary.net/definition/2297/agilitas-agilitatis. Accessed on 5 May 2021

McKinsey (2021) Building workforce skills at scale to thrive during—and after—the COVID-19 crisis. https://www.mckinsey.com/business-functions/organization/our-insights/building-workforce-skills-at-scale-to-thrive-during-and-after-the-covid-19-crisis. Accessed on 06 May 2021

Nagel NR (1992) 21st century manufacturing enterprise strategy report. Iacocca Institute Lehigh University, AMEF N0001-92, Prepared for the Office of Naval Research Arlington, VA

Nkuda MO (2017) Strategic agility and competitive advantage: exploration of the ontological, epistemological and theoretical underpinnings. Br J Econ Manage Trade 16(1):1–13. Article no.BJEMT.30979. ISSN: 2278-098X

Oyedijo A (2012) Strategic agility and competitive performance in the Nigerian telecommunication industry: an empirical investigation. Am Int J Contemp Res 2(3):227–237

Raj KH, Verma AK, Dwivedi SN, Patvardhan C, Mishra DS, Sharma RS (2012) Agile manufacturing systems: approach for enhancing agility of organisations and processes. [N.p.]: Narosa Publishing House Pvt. Ltd. https://search.ebscohost.com/login.aspx?direct=true&db=nlebk&AN=2155237&lang=tr&site=eds-live&scope=site

Sampath G, Bhattacharyya SS, Krishnamoorty B (2021) Microfoundations approach to strategic agility—exploration to operationalization. J General Manage 46(2):103–128. https://doi.org/10.1177/0306307020939359

Sharifi H, Zhang Z (1999) A methodology for achieving agility in manufacturing organisations: an introduction. Int J Prod Econ 62(1):7–22

Sherehiy B, Karwowski W, Layer JK (2007) A review of enterprise agility: concepts, frameworks, and attributes. Int J Ind Ergon 37(5):445–460

Sine WD, Mitsuhashi H, Kirsch DA (2006) Revisting burns and stalker: formal structure and new venture performance in emerging economic sectors. Acad Manage J 49(1):121–132

Uğurlu YÖ, Çolakoğlu E, Öztosun E (2019) The Effect of Strategic Agility on Firm Performance: A Research in Manufacturing Firms. İş ve İnsan Dergisi | The Journal of Human and Work Yıl|Year: Nisan|April 2019 Cilt-Sayı 6(1):93–106. e-ISSN 2148–967X. https://doi.org/10.18394/iid.492829

Yusuf YY, Sarhadi M, Gunesekaran A (1999) Agile manufacturing: the drivers, concept and attributes. Int J Product Econ, 33–43

Chapter 4
Field Study to Evaluate the Effect of Strategic Leadership and Organizational Ambidexterity on Organizational Agility

Abstract Today's dynamism has brought agility into question in business life, and considering the studies on this subject both in the corporate and academic world, it is possible to say that organizations need dynamic capabilities in the face of change. Managing different processes developing under the changing conditions requires different leadership skills. In other words, leaders having the ability to act in accordance with circumstances are needed. Considering that strategic leaders having these characteristics can both benefit from the resources within the organization in the most efficient way (exploitative) and carry out dynamic strategies that include innovative approaches (exploratory) in a balanced way (ambidexterity), the idea that achieving and maintaining organizational ambidexterity as well can be considered as a dynamic skill, shaped our research. Starting from this point of view, in our study, we investigated the effect of strategic leaders and organizational ambidexterity, which we see as a dynamic capability in achieving organizational agility. The research has been conducted on the first 500 Large Enterprises determined every year by the Istanbul Chamber of Industry (ICI) (Turkey) and 500 medium-sized enterprises with different fields of activity, which are selected from the geographical regions in which these companies operate. The data obtained from the research (339 valid questionnaires) were analyzed with Structural Equation Modeling (SEM) by applying Confirmatory Factor Analysis. While it has been seen that different dimensions of strategic leadership and organizational ambidexterity have a direct positive effect on some dimensions of organizational agility, it has been observed that the dimension of ethical strategic leadership has a direct and reverse effect on organizational agility dimensions. At the same time, it has been determined that organizational ambidexterity has a mediating role in the relationship between strategic leadership and some sub-dimensions of organizational ambidexterity.

Keywords Organizational mastery · Dynamic capabilities · Organizational ambidexterity · Field study · Structural equation modelling

İ. Kumkale, *Organizational Mastery*, Accounting, Finance, Sustainability, Governance & Fraud: Theory and Application, https://doi.org/10.1007/978-981-16-7582-9_4

4.1 The Purpose and Importance of the Research

In order for organizations to adapt to developing and changing conditions and to gain competitive advantage, it is highly important to be flexible, to respond quickly to customer demands and to have the competencies to provide them, that is, to become an agile organization. Arokodare and Asikhia (2020) stated that agility increases organizational performance and suggested to organization managers to adopt strategic agility in order to achieve superior performance such as market share, company profitability, company productivity, competitive advantage, customer satisfaction and company creativity. This is because agile organizations provide competitive advantage in terms of speed, flexibility, innovation, proactivity, quality, profitability, customer orientation, transparency, cooperation, entrepreneurship. The dynamism in today's business life has drawn attention to the issue of agility in both the corporate and academic world (Harsch and Festing 2020). When considered in this context, it is possible to say that organizations also need dynamic capabilities in the face of change. Starting from this point of view, in our study, we have investigated the effect of strategic leaders and organizational ambidexterity, which we see as a dynamic capability in achieving organizational agility. Managing different processes which develop when the conditions change requires different leadership skills. In other words, leaders with the ability to act according to circumstances are needed.

With the idea that strategic leaders with these characteristics can both benefit from the resources within the organization in the most efficient way (exploitative) and execute dynamic strategies that include innovative approaches (exploratory) in a balanced way (ambidexterity), and the reflection of achieving and maintaining organizational duality can also be considered as a dynamic skill shaped our research.

Considering the conditions in the business world today, we think that both the content of our study and the results of our research will provide benefit for organizations. On the other hand, it is thought that it will contribute to the studies of academicians as an empirical research on organizational ambidexterity and organizational agility, which has not yet been adequately researched, especially during the Covid 19 Pandemic period.

4.2 Brief Theoretical Background on the Relationship of Research Variables

In this section, brief information will be given about the dynamic capabilities theory, which is the basis of our research, and literature studies on the relations of the variables that are the subject of the research will be mentioned.

4.2.1 *Research-Based Dynamic Capabilities Theory that Forms the Basis of Research*

The dynamic capabilities theory, which drew attention in the field of strategic management with the publication of the article "Dynamic Capabilities and Strategic Management", by Teece et al., in the Strategic Management Journal in 1997, took part in shaping our research. In this study, the authors claim that businesses should develop dynamic capabilities in order to gain competitive advantage and maintain this advantage, especially in dynamic/turbulent environmental conditions. They defined dynamic capabilities as "the company's ability to integrate, create and restructure internal and external qualifications to handle rapidly changing environments (Teece et al. 1997). According to Teece, understanding the issue of competition and wealth creation lies at the heart of the "Dynamic Capabilities" management theory (Teece 2009).

Dynamic capabilities relate to the inimitable capacity of businesses to reshape and/or reconfigure assets again and again when needed, to respond to changing technologies and markets. It involves perceiving, addressing and adapting to the changes related to the internal and external environment in the environment in which the businesses operate, and even developing the skills to have a say in this issue and creating competencies. Dynamic capabilities govern the rate of change of the normal abilities. Although a business has the chance to provide a competitive return for a short time with its resources and savings, this superiority cannot be sustained if it does not have dynamic capabilities. This is because; dynamic capabilities include the capacity of enterprises to interpret the uncertainty correctly and bring it to the appropriate values with the most appropriate tolerances, to achieve continuous, effective and corporate management (Teece 2009). In order for the organization to acquire effective and dynamic talents, it must be versatile, and it requires a high-level leadership that includes duality, cognitive and behavioral flexibility in accordance with Teece's triple classification as perception, capture and restructuring (Xiaoyan et al. 2015).

4.2.2 *Organizational Ambidexterity—Strategic Leadership*

As in many issues, the rapid change emerging in the markets causes organizations to make more effort and search for their survival and sustainability than before. Organizations need to both make the best use of the opportunities they have and be ready for the future. It is not enough for the managers of the organizations to apply approaches that keep the current situation, they also need to adopt and implement an innovative and proactive approach for the future. While underutilize of the assets the organization owns lays the groundwork for the current image and reputation of the organization to be shaken, lack of the ability to prepare for the future may lead to worrisome consequences for the future for the organization. The inability of many reputable organizations, which had a positive image before their customers and other stakeholders in the past, to use exploitative and explorative strategies together, causes them to lose their old reputation and positive image or to be swept out from the market (Bakan et al. 2019).

In order to be ambidexter, organizations must be able to reconcile the conflicting demands and internal tensions between units/individuals in their internal working environments. While there were studies that stated that these tradeoffs were insurmountable before, studies that support ambidexterity and provide institutional solutions for the development of this skill, as well as studies that explore leadership characteristics that allow organizations to manage the contradictions they encounter have begun.

Besides the work of Gibson and Birkinshaw in 2004, which draws attention to the important role played by senior managers in making the context of the organization effective and developing ambidexterity, and the work of Smith and Tushman in 2005 on integrative mechanisms by which leadership teams can successfully manage the conflicts arising from structural separation in ambidextrous organizations (Raisch and Birkinshaw 2008), in many studies on organizational ambidexterity, it has been emphasized that leadership characteristics, composition and leadership processes are also important in the application of structural and contextual ambidexterity (Sinha 2015; Gibson and Birkinshaw 2004; Lubatkin et al. 2006; Staub and Arslan 2017). It has been stated that the role of leaders at the top of the organization and business unit is highly influential in designing an effective context for the practice of ambidexterity. Some researchers also argue that managers became the central to "mediating between the forces of convergence and the forces of change" (Tushman and Romanelli 1985).

Malewska and Sajdak (2014) stated that Ford, Microsoft, Apple or Polsat owe their success to their founders, Henry Ford, Bill Gates, Steve Jobs and Zygmunt Solorz Żak, and that the success of their companies even cannot be imagined without them. According to them, the success or failure of a company depends on its leader, therefore how strategic leadership is perceived and applied is very important. A broad business vision (often initially an unrealistic vision) is one of the common characteristics seen in all of these founders, including full use of business resources (exploitative) and potential for development (exploratory).

As contexts change, with the proliferation of complexity and ambiguity, a need has arisen for leaders who are creative rather than adaptive, capable of analysis and synthesis, and capable of performing a multidimensional set of actions; because such environments require leaders who show agility of mind and action (Pisapia and Ying 2011).

Pisapia (2006) states that, while the strategic leaders manage the current situation (exploratory) on the one hand, they also direct the organization to a new future (exploitative). He propounds that strategic leaders use a palette of managerial, transformative, political and ethical actions to guide the organization through the maze of change, just as Leonardo da Vinci used his perspective window, and make continuous and conscious choices between these four sets of actions (We see this as a dynamic talent, and consider it as the strategic leader's ability to manage the internal and external environment of the organization in a balanced way). In Leonardo's perspective interpretation, there is a quest not only to depict what appears on the scene, but also to make invisible objects visible. He transforms his works into artistic works with his different skills of using his brush, creating dream-like effects consisting of softening the edges, blurring the shadows, light coming from the shadows, atmospheric fog and haze. According to Pisapia, Leonardo's window presents several lessons for strategic leaders. First, they must be able to pause, feel and enter the "moment", second, seek the invisible and find things that are not in the current picture but belong there, and third, recognize new possibilities and paths in a chartless terrain. Similarly, the leaders must use a multifaceted set of actions that they blend with a coordinated effort to achieve a goal. Understanding which action will be effective in which situation requires balance and intuition. In his 2006 study, Pisapia compared applying transformative, managerial, political, and ethical leadership skills in an integrative way to an artist using his palette with paint brushes, to putting on Superman's cape. A few years later (2009 and 2011) he added *communication skill* to these skills as the fifth (Pisapia and Ying 2011).

In Pisapia's opinion, strategic leadership is not just the task of top management. Leaders at every important intersection in organizations must be able to work strategically. One of the basic principles of his strategic leadership theory is that, the leaders who can think and act with agility can create more supportive organizational conditions and achieve more valuable organizational results (http://thestrategicleader.org/content/principles-strategic-leadership-0, 20.06.2020).

4.2.3 Organizational Agility—Strategic Leadership

There have been many studies examining the effects of strategic thinking, strategic agility and strategic management on the performance of companies and creating competitive advantage. For example, Salih and Alnaji (2014), in their studies, determined that strategic thinking and strategic agility affect strategic performance, and that strategic agility also plays an intermediary role in developing and strengthening performance. Oyedijo (2012) propounded in his study that strategic agility has a significant effect on competitive performance, with the example of telecommunications companies; he suggested that their managers develop organizational, human resource, technological and planning qualifications and practices that can make their companies' agile in order for the companies to survive, grow, and compete effectively in both national and regional markets.

Enterprises developing agile products concordant to meet the current conditions and consumer demands, as well as find agile business models gain a competitive advantage in the market. Ileri and Soylu think that, the success of small but agile companies can be attributed to their efforts in this way. It is seen that, providing a competitive advantage of agility has also started to change the traditionally expressed assumption of "big fish eat small fish" and that giant companies of a period could not adapt themselves to new conditions and disappeared. In the OECD's research, it is emphasized that in order to be long-lasting, for businesses acting "quickly" and responding "quickly" to economic conditions is important (Ileri and Soylu 2014).

Ustasüleyman (2008), in his research, investigated the effects of changes in production technologies, information technologies, market, competition criteria and social factors, which are expressed as the compellers of agility, the increase in the importance of products manufactured upon order and global competition, and the effect of competitive capacity, which eliminates the effect of agility compellers on the performance of the enterprise. As the competitive capacity criteria (cited by Ileri and Soylu 2014), determination of options together with customers, production volume flexibility, low cost, rapid action in the market with new products, internal and external cooperation, model and configuration flexibility in product, quality, speed of delivery in production have been taken as the basis. According to the results of the research conducted by interviewing 128 companies; it was determined that agility compellers have a positive and significant effect on business performance; in regard to the prominent competitive capacity factors, leadership in new technology and the ability to compete quickly in the market were identified as the most important measure of competitive capacity.

In order to apply the agile management system and be successful, companies need to have a well-trained workforce, should follow the technological developments and accommodate to their structures very quickly. In addition, talented managers and employees who are prone to teamwork are of great importance in this process (Ileri and Soylu 2014). Crocitto and Youssef (2003) also stated that agility will emerge when it is supported by the leader as a value and strategy of the organization.

Harvard Business Review Turkey and ACM Agile Consulting Company made their second e-book on Agility in November 2020, and discussed the subject of "Agile Management", they asked the question "Are you Ready for Agile Transformation?" in an environment where the momentum of change is on increasing in a period of uncertainty prevalence. In the e-book, which includes many studies on these topics, and in the study titled "Embracing Agility" by Rigby et al. (2020), the sample practices demonstrated the importance of agile teams and senior management. It is important that working with agile teams lead the organization to success, but it should also not be overlooked that it is the top management and the leader of the organization who decides to establish agile teams, successfully carries out their working processes, and thus enables the organization to implement agile practices.

As it is seen in the studies in the field of management and for many reasons given above, being an agile organization is becoming more and more important. In addition to many factors that can make organizations agile, it can be said that the leader of the organization is the primary factor that can be expressed basically. It is thought that strategic leadership competencies are needed for the organization's ability to efficiently and effectively manage its own material assets and capabilities, to see and evaluate the opportunities that develop around it before anyone else, to notice and eliminate the upcoming or potential threats before their competitors, if they cannot eliminate them to try not to be affected, and to be very fast and flexible in the whole process.

4.3 Population and Sample

The universe of the research consists of the first 500 Large Enterprises (enterprises on the ISO—Istanbul Chamber of Industry (2019 list) determined every year by the Istanbul Chamber of Industry (ISO) (Turkey) and 500 Medium-Sized Enterprises with different fields of activity, which are selected easily by sampling from the geographical areas in which these companies operate.

The data obtained from the research were analyzed with Structural Equation Modeling (SEM) by applying Confirmatory Factor Analysis. SEM is a method used for multivariate data analysis in experimental and non-experimental research where both observable and unobservable variables can be tested at the same time, direct and indirect multiple relationships or consecutive indirect relationships can be measured (Karagöz 2019; Werner and Schermelleh-Engel 2009; Byrne 2010). Bayram (2010) stated that there is not much clarity in the literature about sample size for SEM applications, and propounded that, since the structural equation models of some authors like Kline, 2005; Harrington, 2009 are based on tests sensitive to the significance of the differences in the covariance matrix and sample size, those authors thought that the sample size should not be small when establishing such models. He expressed that, as a rough measure, those authors are considering a sample size of less than 100 can be defined as small, a sample size of 100–200 can be defined as medium, and a sample size of more than 200 can be defined as large sample volumes in general. To the way of authors' thinking, small sample sizes can be suitable for very simple models while medium sample sizes are suitable for not so much complex models and large volume samples are convenient for complex ones. He also stated that, while some of the researchers point out a sample size of 200–400 sample size for 10–15 indicator variables, the sample sizes of some other researchers on the other hand, are at least chosen between 100 and 200, and in many surveys 250–500 sample size are being used (Bayram 2010). In our study, since 1000 enterprises accepted as the population, with 99% confidence level and 5% error the sample size (https://www.surveysystem.com/sscalc.htm) determined as 400. The return amount of the surveys forming the research sample in accordance with the enterprises was 358 (35.8%). But the questionnaire forms which were filled incorrectly and missing deducted and 339 questionnaires are included in the analysis.

$$n = \frac{NZ^2P(1-P)}{d^2(N-1)+Z^2P(1-P)} = \frac{(1000)(2,58)^2(0,50)(0,50)}{(0,05)^2(1000-1)+(2.58)^2(0,50)(0,50)} = 399$$

Error Margin d = 0.05, P: Possibility of Success, Z = %99 Confidence Interval

4.4 Constraints of the Research

Conducting the research during the Covid-19 Pandemic period was beneficial in terms of obtaining important information about the subject we studied, but for the same reason, it prevented the questionnaires, which were the data collection tool of the research, from being filled with face-to-face interviews. The questionnaires were prepared via Google Form and sent on-line to the e-mail addresses obtained from the official websites of the companies. Due to the firewalls in the systems of some enterprises, they could not be delivered to the companies and the mails were returned. On the other hand, it is thought that the managers are reluctant to fill in the questionnaires because they are requested to fill in the questionnaires and they have very high time limits. Due to aforementioned reasons, although the number of people who answered the questionnaire is known, it is not clear how many managers from how many companies filled out the forms.

4.5 Data Collection Method and Scales Used in the Research

The data obtained in the research consists of primary and secondary data. Secondary data were acquired from the sources such as national and international articles, books, reports, etc. that have been obtained as a result of the literature review on the subject. The primary data, on the other hand, was obtained from the questionnaire forms sent to the companies and returned after being answered.

Forming of the questionnaires to be used for the research, previously developed, validity and reliability tested scales were used. Three different scales were used to measure the dependent and independent variables in the model developed for the research. The scales are scales adapted to Turkish as 5-point Likert type scales. The evaluation of proposals have been arranged as "1 = Strongly Disagree, 2 = Disagree, 3 = Neither Agree Nor Disagree), 4 = Agree, 5 = Strongly Agree". There were 25 statements in Strategic Leadership Scale, 20 statements in Organizational Ambidexterity Scale, 17 statements in Organizational Agility Scale. In addition, 9 questions were included in the questionnaire to determine the demographic characteristics of the participants. Ethics Committee Approval Report (Appendix B) was received for the arranged and finalized questionnaire (Appendix A).

Conducting the questionnaire of the study was made by sending the link of the survey forms (https://docs.google.com/forms/d/e/1FAIpQLSfbzl4ubbgcPEbHEjm-QHwoc2uWzdtCeAVa3KRL2VOve4FmcQ/viewform?vc=0&c=0&w=1&flr=0&gxids=7628) prepared electronically on Google Form to the companies via e-mail. In particular, top, middle and lower level managers in managerial positions were asked to fill out the form. The number and percentage of the Questionnaire forms answered and sent from managers working at different levels were 358 (47%).

Table 4.1 Dimensions of strategic leadership scale

Dimensions of strategic leadership	Statements
Managerial strategic leadership	1–5
Transformative strategic leadership	6–10
Political strategic leadership	11–15
Communicative leadership	16–20
Ethical leadership	21–25
Total	25

4.5.1 *Strategic Leadership Scale*

To measure the strategic leadership levels of managers, The Strategic Leadership Questionnaire (SLQ), developed by Pisapia (Pisapia, 2009; Pisapia and Ying, 2011) and adapted into Turkish by Aydın (2012), was used in the study. It was arranged in the form of five point Likert, comprising the dimensions of transformative, ethical, political, managerial and communicative strategic leadership behaviors. The scale used was first developed by Pisapia (2006) as four dimensions (managerial, transformational, political and ethical dimensions) and has been used in many studies. It was rearranged as five dimensions in 2009 and changed the titles of the dimensions as managing, transforming, bonding (ethical), bridging (communicative) and bartering (political) (Pisapia and Ying 2011). The contents of the dimensions were explained in 2.1.4. In our study, it was preferred to express the dimensions as follows (Table 4.1).

4.5.2 *Organizational Ambidexterity Scale*

In our study, organizational ambidexterity was examined in two dimensions: structural ambidexterity and contextual ambidexterity. Structural ambidexterity is a 5-point Likert-type scale with 14 statements prepared by Jansen et al. (2006), considered in two sub-dimensions as exploratory innovative ability and exploitative/developer innovative ability (Table 4.2). In the adaptation of the scale into Turkish, which its permissions were received for the research, first it was translated by the researcher, then it was translated back into English by an English-trained academician, and then again it was translated back into Turkish by an academician

Table 4.2 Dimensions of structural ambidexterity scale

Structural ambidexterity scale	Statements
Exploratory innovative ability	1–7
Exploitative/developer innovative ability	8–14
Total	14

Table 4.3 Dimensions of contextual ambidexterity scale

Contextual ambidexterity scale	Statements
Alignment	15–17
Adaptability	18–20
Total	6

who has mastered in the body of literature, finally the scale was given its final form by the researcher after reviewing the translations of the researchers previously used the same scale.

The contextual ambidexterity scale was also developed by Gibson and Birkinshaw (2004) by considering it in two sub-dimensions. This scale is also a 5-point Likert-type scale consisting of a total of 6 statements, and it has been prepared in a way 3 statements to measure adaptation and 3 statements to measure adaptability (Table 4.3). The permissions of the scale were received and the process in adaptation of the scale into Turkish, similar to structural ambidexterity scale of Jansen et al., actualized by the same academicians, and the final form of the scale was arranged by the researcher.

4.5.3 *Organizational Agility Scale*

For measuring organizational agility, Organizational Agility Scale which has been developed by Sharifi and Zhang (1999) and adapted into Turkish by Akkaya and Tabak (2018) was used. Both for the original scale and the scale's version adapted into Turkish, the permissions for use have been received. Scale consists of four sub-dimensions (Competence, Flexibility, Responsiveness, Speed/Quickness) and 17 5-point Likert type entries (Table 4.4).

4.6 Research Model and Hypotheses

A conceptual model (Fig. 4.1.) and research hypotheses were developed in the context of this model, based on the literature information given in the first, second and

Table 4.4 Dimensions of organizational agility scale

Organizational agility scale	Statements
Competence	1–8
Flexibility	9–11
Responsiveness	12–14
Speed/quickness	15–17
Total	17

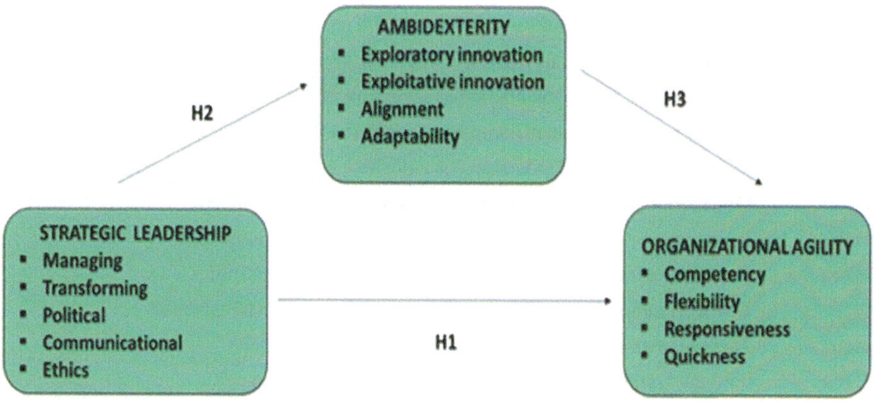

Fig. 4.1 Conceptual model of the research

third parts of the study and also the information under the title of the purpose and importance of the research in the fourth (4.1. and 4.2) part (Table 4.5).

4.7 Structural Equation Modeling Assumptions

There is no consensus among the related researchers about the minimum sample size in Structural Equation Modeling (SEM) studies. Analyzes in which all outcome variables are in a permanent form and normally distributed, all effects are linear, and there is no interaction between variables, require smaller sample sizes than analyzes where some variables are non-continuous, do not show normal distribution, or show curvilinear or interacting characteristics (Kline 2019). However, as a general rule, confirmatory factor analysis and SEM analysis are not considered appropriate for data below 150 (Gürbüz 2019).

In SEM, it is important that the data set has a multivariate normal distribution. There are several methods used to study multivariate normality. When the distribution deviates from normality, data transformation is applied to bring it closer to the normal distribution. As a result of data transformation, it is seen that other assumptions are met and the accuracy of statistical analysis results is ensured (Çokluk et al. 2012). Another method used in data where multivariate normality cannot be achieved is the "bootstrap" method. It operates as a resampling technique that is considered representative of the original data. Data is provided for empirical analysis of parameter estimation and fit indices over the repeated samples taken randomly from the original sample (with replacement) (Byrne 2010). In the bootstrap approach, parameters, standard errors and model test statistics are estimated by empirical sampling distributions from a large number of produced samples (Çokluk et al. 2012; cited by Demiralay 2014). In the study, the bootstrap method, which was suggested as

Table 4.5 Research hypotheses

H1	*Strategic leadership has a positive effect on organizational agility*
H1aa	Managerial strategic leadership has a positive effect on competence
H1ab	Managerial strategic leadership has a positive effect on flexibility
H1ac	Managerial strategic leadership has a positive effect on responsiveness
H1ad	Managerial strategic leadership has a positive effect on speed
H1ba	Transformational leadership has a positive effect on competence
H1bb	Transformational leadership has a positive effect on flexibility
H1bc	Transformational leadership has a positive effect on responsiveness
H1bd	Transformational leadership has a positive effect on speed
H1ca	Political leadership has a positive effect on competence
H1cb	Political leadership has a positive effect on flexibility
H1cc	Political leadership has a positive effect on responsiveness
H1cd	Political leadership has a positive effect on speed
H1da	Ethical leadership has a positive effect on competence
H1db	Ethical leadership has a positive effect on flexibility
H1dc	Ethical leadership has a positive effect on responsiveness
H1dd	Ethical leadership has a positive effect on speed
H1ea	Communicative leadership has a positive effect on competence
H1eb	Communicative leadership has a positive effect on flexibility
H1ec	Communicative has a positive effect on responsiveness
H1ed	Communicative leadership has a positive effect on speed
H2	*Strategic leadership has a positive effect on organizational ambidexterity*
H2aa	Managerial strategic leadership has a positive effect on explorative innovation ambidexterity
H2ab	Managerial strategic leadership has a positive effect on exploitative innovation ambidexterity
H2ac	Managerial strategic leadership has a positive effect on alignment ability
H2ad	Managerial strategic leadership has a positive effect on adaptability
H2ba	Transformational strategic leadership has a positive effect on explorative innovation ambidexterity
H2bb	Transformational strategic leadership has a positive effect on exploitative innovation ambidexterity
H2bc	Transformational strategic leadership has a positive effect on alignment ability
H2bd	Transformational strategic leadership has a positive effect on adaptability
H2ca	Political strategic leadership has a positive effect on explorative innovation ambidexterity
H2cb	Political strategic leadership has a positive effect on exploitative innovation ambidexterity
H2cc	Political strategic leadership has a positive effect on alignment ability

(continued)

Table 4.5 (continued)

H2cd	Political strategic leadership has a positive effect on adaptability
H2da	Ethical strategic leadership has a positive effect on explorative innovation ambidexterity
H2db	Ethical strategic leadership has a positive effect on exploitative innovation ambidexterity
H2dc	Ethical strategic leadership has a positive effect on alignment
H2dd	Ethical strategic leadership has a positive effect on adaptability
H2ea	Communicative strategic leadership has a positive effect on explorative innovation ambidexterity
H2eb	Communicative strategic leadership has a positive effect on exploitative innovation ambidexterity
H2ec	Communicative strategic leadership has a positive effect on alignment
H2ed	Communicative strategic leadership has a positive effect on adaptability
H3	*Organizational ambidexterity has a positive effect on strategic agility*
H3aa	Explorative innovation ambidexterity has a positive effect on competence
H3ab	Explorative innovation ambidexterity has a positive effect on flexibility
H3ac	Explorative innovation ambidexterity has a positive effect on responsiveness
H3ad	Explorative innovation ambidexterity has a positive effect on speed
H3ba	Exploitative innovation ambidexterity has a positive effect on competence
H3bb	Exploitative innovation ambidexterity has a positive effect on flexibility
H3bc	Exploitative innovation ambidexterity has a positive effect on responsiveness
H3bd	Exploitative innovation ambidexterity has a positive effect on speed
H3ca	Alignment has a positive effect on competence
H3cb	Alignment has a positive effect on flexibility
H3cc	Alignment has a positive effect on responsiveness
H3cd	Alignment has a positive effect on speed
H3da	Adaptability has a positive effect on competency
H3db	Adaptability has a positive effect on flexibility
H3dc	Adaptability has a positive effect on responsiveness
H3dd	Adaptability has a positive effect on speed
H4	*Organizational ambidexterity has a mediating role in the relationship between strategic leadership and organizational agility*
H4aa	Organizational ambidexterity has a mediating role in the relationship between managerial strategic leadership and competency
H4ab	Organizational ambidexterity has a mediating role in the relationship between managerial strategic leadership and flexibility
H4ac	Organizational ambidexterity has a mediating role in the relationship between managerial strategic leadership and responsiveness
H4ad	Organizational ambidexterity has a mediating role in the relationship between managerial strategic leadership and speed

(continued)

Table 4.5 (continued)

H4ba	Organizational ambidexterity has a mediating role in the relationship between transformative strategic leadership and competency
H4bb	Organizational ambidexterity has a mediating role in the relationship between transformative strategic leadership and flexibility
H4bc	Organizational ambidexterity has a mediating role in the relationship between transformative strategic leadership and responsiveness
H4bd	Organizational ambidexterity has a mediating role in the relationship between transformative strategic leadership and speed
H4ca	Organizational ambidexterity has a mediating role in the relationship between political strategic leadership and competency
H4cb	Organizational ambidexterity has a mediating role in the relationship between political strategic leadership and flexibility
H4cc	Organizational ambidexterity has a mediating role in the relationship between political strategic leadership and responsiveness
H4cd	Organizational ambidexterity has a mediating role in the relationship between political strategic leadership and speed
H4da	Organizational ambidexterity has a mediating role in the relationship between communicative strategic leadership and competency
H4db	Organizational ambidexterity has a mediating role in the relationship between communicative strategic leadership and flexibility
H4dc	Organizational ambidexterity has a mediating role in the relationship between communicative strategic leadership and responsiveness
H4dd	Organizational ambidexterity has a mediating role in the relationship between communicative strategic leadership and speed
H4ea	Organizational ambidexterity has a mediating role in the relationship between ethical strategic leadership and competency
H4eb	Organizational ambidexterity has a mediating role in the relationship between ethical strategic leadership and flexibility
H4ec	Organizational ambidexterity has a mediating role in the relationship between ethical strategic leadership and responsiveness
H4ed	Organizational ambidexterity has a mediating role in the relationship between ethical strategic leadership and speed

an auxiliary method, was applied to the data that did not provide the normality assumption.

4.8 Findings of the Research

In this section, information about the socio-demographic characteristics of the respondents will be included, analysis and findings regarding the scales will be presented, and the results will be evaluated by testing the research model.

4.8.1 Socio-demographical Characteristics of the Respondents

Information on the demographic and socio-economic characteristics of the company managers participating in the research is given in Table 4.6. As seen in the table, the participants were asked about their gender, age, education level, tenure in the company they are currently working in, tenure in the profession, their current title, the sector in which the company operates and the size of the company, and the number of activities they participated on the issues related to their profession. Information containing each of the related topics is given in separate graphs (Figs. 4.2, 4.3, 4.4, 4.5, 4.6, 4.7, 4.8, 4.9 and 4.10).

When the gender distribution of the managers participating in the survey (Fig. 4.2) is examined, it is seen that 1/3 of the total managers are female managers, with a rate of 72.60% male managers are twice as many as female managers (27.40%).

Looking at Fig. 4.3, it is seen that people in managerial positions are mostly between the ages of 31–50 (69.9%). It is seen that there are managers over the age of 60 in a remarkable small proportion. Besides, 12.10% managers are under the age of 30. In general, it can be said that young managers are the managers of successful businesses.

It is seen that the education level of the participants who are in the managerial position and who responded to our survey is 97.9% of the university education. 21.9% of this is at master's and doctorate level. The fact that 2.1% of the participants are high school graduates and rise to a managerial position can be interpreted as a career opportunity in their company is offered if they are successful (Fig. 4.4).

Figure 4.5 shows the tenure of the managers in the company. When the graph is examined, it is seen that nearly half of the managers (45%) have been working in the same company for more than 15 years. When we consider the time worked in the enterprise as more than 10 years, the rate rises to an important level of 60.3%. This situation may indicate that the managers do not think of moving to a different business after coming to a certain management position in the business. Employees between 0 and 5 years, which can be spelled the shortest time, constitute approximately ¼ of the managers with a rate of 23.9%. It is seen that there is no necessity to work in the enterprise for a very long time in order to take a managerial position.

When the seniority of the managers is examined (Fig. 4.6), it is seen that approximately 75% of them have more than 10 years of professional experience, and 11.2% of them are the young managers who have just started their business life. 25% of managers have less than 10 years of professional experience.

When the levels of management in the companies of the respondents are examined; it is seen that 18% are senior managers, 37.5% are middle level managers, and 39.8% are junior level managers. It is understood that some of the managers are the owners or shareholders of the company and they also carry on business at the management level (4.7%) (Fig. 4.7).

Table 4.6 Socio-demographical characteristics of the Respondents

Gender	Frequency	%
Female	93	27.4
Male	246	72.6
Age		
Between 20 and 30	41	12.1
Between 31 and 40	110	32.4
Between 41 and 50	127	37.5
Between 51 and 60	57	16.8
61+	4	1.2
Education level		
High school	7	2.1
Associate degree	28	8.3
Bachelor's degree	230	67.8
Postgraduate degree	68	20.1
Doctorate degree	6	1.8
Your tenure in this company		
0–5 years	81	23.9
6–10 years	54	15.9
11–15 years	52	15.3
16–20 years	62	18.3
20+ years	90	26.5
Your tenure in this profession		
0–15 years	38	11.2
6–10 years	48	14.2
11–15 years	58	17.1
16–20 years	72	21,2
20+ years	123	36.3
Your title in this company		
Senior level manager	61	18.0
Middle level manager	127	37.5
Junior level manager	135	39.8
Company owner/shareholder	16	4.7
Sector in which your company operates		
Manufacturing sector	206	60.8
Service industry	98	28.9
Commerce sector	35	10.3
Size of your company		
Large-scale enterprise	283	83.5

(continued)

Table 4.6 (continued)

Gender	Frequency	%
Medium-scale enterprise	56	16.5
Number of in-service activities related to your profession		
1–5	49	14.5
6–10	64	18.9
11–15	48	14.2
16–20	47	13.9
21+	131	38.6

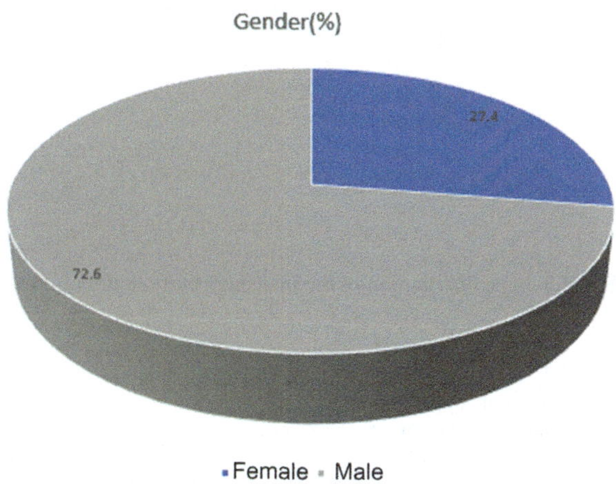

Fig. 4.2 Gender distribution of the managers participating in the survey

When the companies participating in our study were asked about their fields of activity (Fig. 4.8), 61% of the companies stated their sector as the manufacturing sector, 29% as the service sector, and 10% as the commerce sector.

It is seen that 83.5% of the company managers who responded to our survey work at large enterprises and 16.5% at medium-sized enterprises (Fig. 4.9).

It is seen that the company managers participating in our study participated in various trainings, with the lowest rate of the managers participating in trainings (1–5) by 14.5%. In addition, 38.6% of the managers stated that they participated in more than 21 trainings and activities. When evaluated in general terms, it can be thought that managers participate in professional activities (Fig. 4.10).

4.8.2 Analysis and Findings for Scales

In this section, descriptive statistics of the research, the results of general reliability analysis of the scales and information about factor analysis are given.

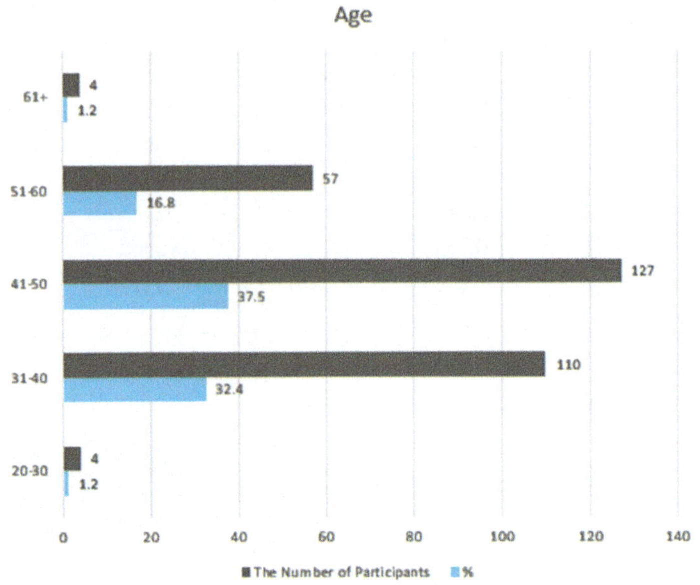

Fig. 4.3 Age distribution of the managers participating in the survey

Fig. 4.4 Education level distribution of the managers participating in the survey

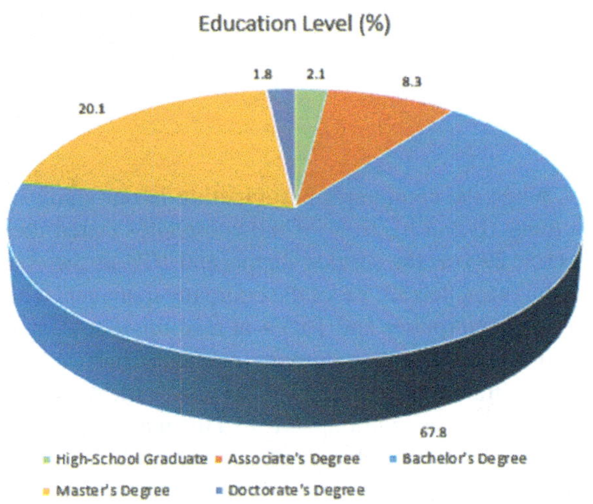

4.8.2.1 Descriptive Statistics

Descriptive statistics for the expressions used in the Strategic Leadership Scale are given in Table 4.7. The general average of the scale expressions is 3.86, and the values vary between 3.09 and 4.21. Standard Deviation also takes values between 0.798 and 1.237.

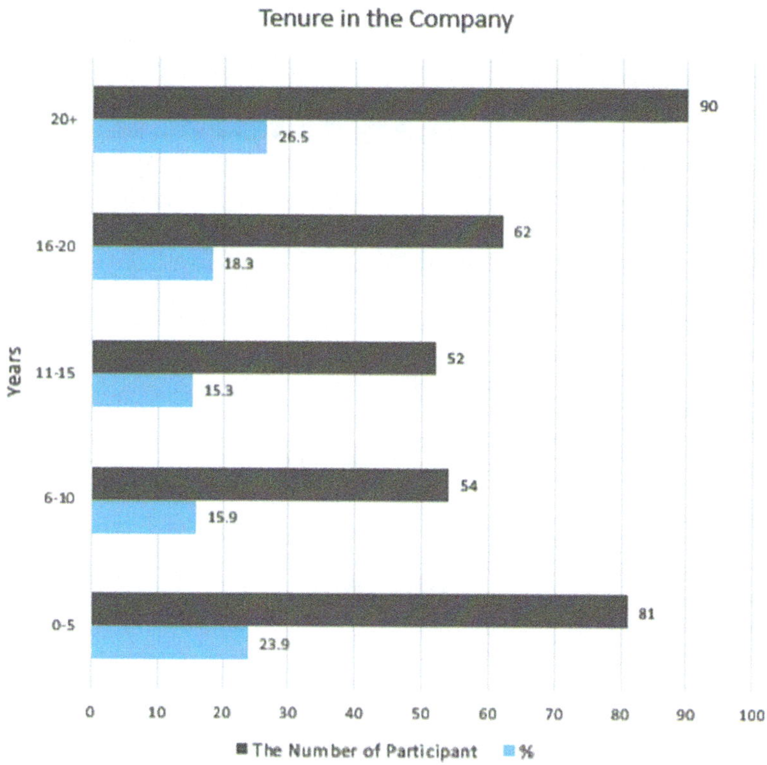

Fig. 4.5 Tenure of the managers participating in the survey in the company

When the highest scores given by the respondents in the dimensions of managerial, transformational, political, communicative and ethical strategic leadership are evaluated; *they state that, the managers hold themselves accountable while fulfilling their obligations (MSL/4.21 points), they emphasize the core values of the organization (TSL/4.05 points) in their interviews with employees and in their decision-making processes. They think that managers are willing to negotiate (PSL/3.86 points) and interact with influential people (CSL/3.98) in the performance of their jobs.* According to them, *their managers respect people's private lives (privacy)* (ESL/4.09 points). When the strategic leadership scale is considered in general, the lowest score was about *managers giving small rewards when they liked the work done* (3.09 points). This score can be interpreted as that the participants did not see a significant level of motivation in this regard.

Descriptive statistics of the expressions used in the organizational duality scale are given in Table 4.8. The general average of the scale expressions is 3.77, and the values vary between 3.26 and 4.24. Standard Deviation also varies between 0.707 and 1.119.

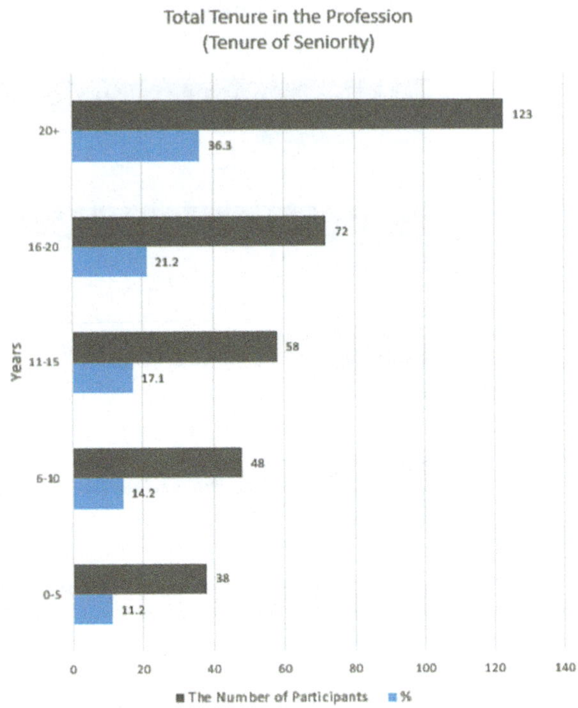

Fig. 4.6 Tenure of the managers participating in the survey in the profession

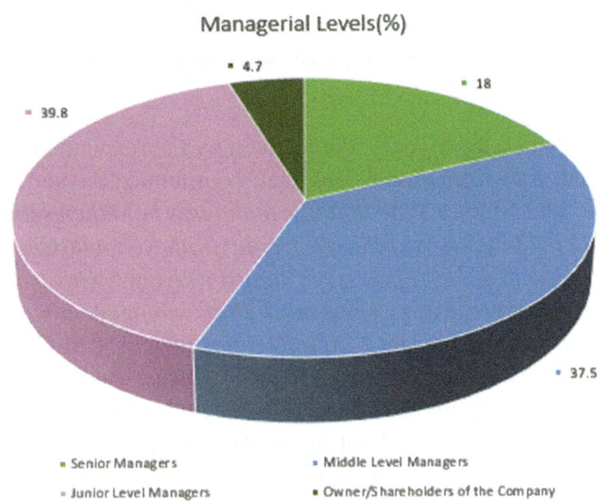

Fig. 4.7 Managerial levels of the managers participating in the survey

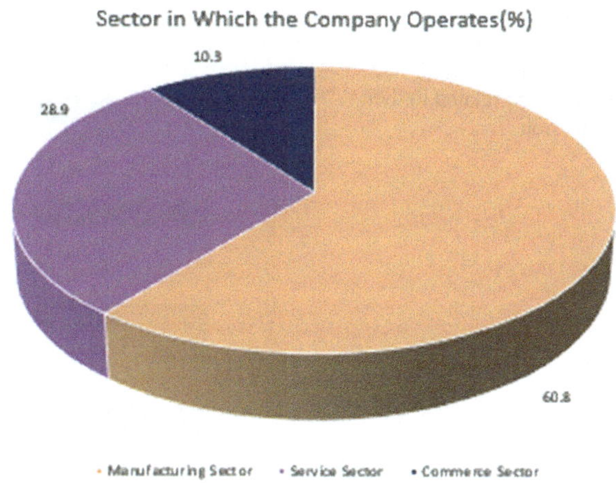

Fig. 4.8 Sector in which the company operates

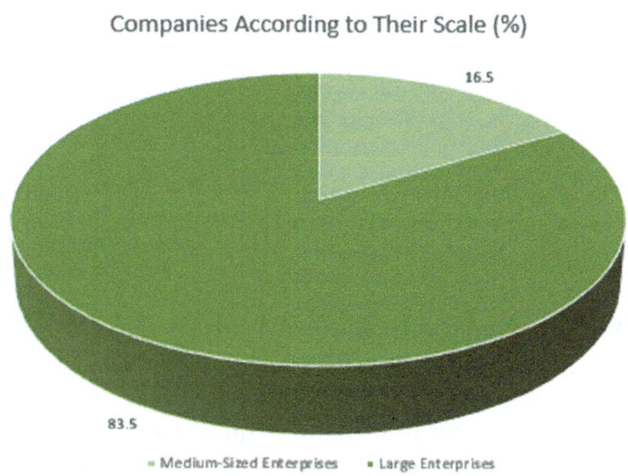

Fig. 4.9 Companies according to their scale

When Table 4.8 is examined, the highest score (4.24) given by the respondents is that *reducing the costs of internal processes is an important goal in their companies.* The second highest score (4.05) was given to the statement that *their companies' management systems work consistently to support all of the firm's objectives.*

Table 4.9 contains descriptive statistics for the expressions used in the organizational agility scale. The general average of the scale expressions is 3.77, and the values vary between 3.55 and 4.25. Standard Deviation also varies between 0.707 and 1.119.

When the answers given to the statements on the organizational agility scale are examined in general, the participants *find the products produced by their companies and the quality of the services they offer to customers high* (4.25 points). They stated that t*heir companies have flexibility in producing different quantities of products and services* (3.78), *they have the ability to respond quickly to changes in customer needs*

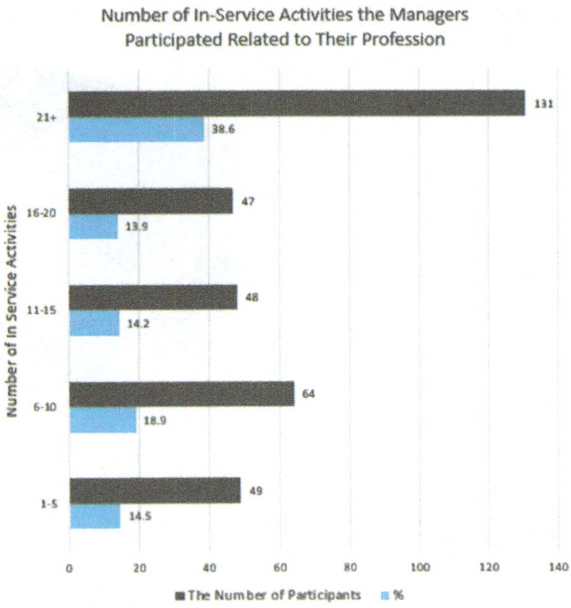

Fig. 4.10 Number of in-service activities the respondent managers participated related to their profession

and preferences (3.82), and *they distribute products and services quickly* (3.91). The lowest score (3.55) was given to *the company's high level of product promotion.*

4.8.2.2 General Reliability Analysis of Scales

To measure the internal consistency of the items included in the scales used in the research and to explain or question the homogeneous structure of the items Cronbach's alpha coefficient is used. It is interpreted that the items in the scale with a high Cronbach's alpha coefficient are consistent with each other, and on the other hand, they consist of items measuring the same feature. Cronbach alpha is frequently used in Likert type scales and is expressed as follows (Yıldız and Uzunsakal 2018):

If $0.00 < \alpha < 0.40$ scale is not reliable.
If $0.40 < \alpha < 0.60$ scale has low reliability.
If $0.60 < \alpha < 0.80$ scale is significantly reliable.
If $0.80 < \alpha < 1.00$ scale is highly reliable.

The "Cronbach's Alpha Coefficient" method was used for the general reliability analyzes of the scales used in the study, and the results are given in Table 4.10. It is seen that the Cronbach Alpha Coefficients of each scale are above 0.60 and reliability of the scales are at the levels of significantly reliable and highly reliable.

Table 4.7 Descriptive statistics on the Items of the strategic leadership scale

Strategic leadership		Strongly disagree	Disagree	Neither agree nor disagree	Agree	Strongly agree	Average	Standard deviation
		f_i $f_i\%$	f_i $f_i\%$	f_i $f_i\%$	f_i $f_i\%$	f_i $f_i\%$	N = 339	
SL1	Our manager decides how things should be done	10 2.9	35 10.3	23 6.8	207 61.1	64 18.9	3.83	0.953
SL2	Our manager enforces rules and policies	9 2.7	19 5.6	12 3.5	210 61.9	89 26.3	4.04	0.873
SL3	Our manager holds us responsible for meeting our obligations	6 1.8	10 2.9	13 3.8	186 54.9	123 36.3	4.21	0.798
SL4	Our manager controls our work	4 1.2	21 6.2	18 5.3	195 57.5	101 29.8	4.09	0.837
SL5	Our manager orders us to follow the chain of command	7 2.1	65 19.2	36 10.6	158 46.6	72 21.2	3.66	1.078
SL6	Our manager encourages us to develop our leadership skills	11 3.2	53 15.6	49 14.5	133 39.2	93 27.4	3.72	1.123
SL7	Our manager encourages employees to adopt the organization's long-term goals	4 1.2	44 13.0	34 10.0	172 50.7	85 25.1	3.86	0.970
SL8	Our manager helps us be aware of opportunities	8 2.4	68 20.1	52 15.3	148 43.7	63 18.6	3.56	1.079
SL9	Our manager strives to create a common vision	4 1.2	42 12.4	34 10.0	174 51.3	85 25.1	3.87	0.968
SL10	Our manager emphasizes the core values of our organization in our discussions and decision-making processes	3 0.9	17 5.0	32 9.4	196 57.8	91 26.8	4.05	0.802
SL11	Our manager is willing to negotiate to get works done	1 0.3	34 10.0	47 13.9	188 55.5	69 20.4	3.86	0.867

(continued)

Table 4.7 (continued)

Strategic leadership		Strongly disagree	Disagree	Neither agree nor disagree	Agree	Strongly agree	Average	Standard deviation
		f_i $f_i\%$	f_i $f_i\%$	f_i $f_i\%$	f_i $f_i\%$	f_i $f_i\%$	N = 339	
SL12	Our manager is ready to compromise to get help when needed	5 1.5	30 8.8	48 14.2	191 56.3	65 19.2	3.83	0.891
SL13	Our manager tries to find win–win solutions (where both sides will benefit) in resolving conflicts	3 0.9	54 15.9	60 17.7	157 46.3	65 19.2	3.67	0.990
SL14	Our manager gives small rewards when he/she likes the good work done	37 10.9	94 27.7	50 14.7	118 34.8	40 11.8	3.09	1.237
SL15	Our manager treats people equally	14 4.1	25 7.4	52 15.3	185 54.6	63 18.6	3.76	0.976
SL16	Our manager involves in an interaction with influential (reputable) people	3 0.9	17 5.0	58 17.1	167 49.3	94 27.7	3.98	0.855
SL17	Our manager works jointly with people outside the organization	6 1.8	39 11.5	67 19.8	144 42.5	83 24.5	3.76	1.007
SL18	Our manager strives to build rapport with people who may have influence on the works get done	4 1.2	32 9.4	44 13.0	179 52.8	80 23.6	3.88	0.915
SL19	Our manager establishes close relationships with influential people	3 0.9	26 7.7	65 19.2	173 51.0	72 21.2	3.84	0.876

(continued)

4.8.2.3 Factor Analysis

Factor analysis analyzes which of the statements in a scale measuring a particular phenomenon are perceived close to each other. It is a statistical method used to bring these variables together in groups by examining the relationship between many variables in the scale (Saruhan and Özdemirci 2013). Briefly, it is the process of

Table 4.7 (continued)

Strategic leadership		Strongly disagree	Disagree	Neither agree nor disagree	Agree	Strongly agree	Average	Standard deviation
		f_i f_i%	f_i f_i%	f_i f_i%	f_i f_i%	f_i f_i%	N = 339	
SL20	Our manager uses his/her connections (like people he/she knows) and communication networks to get works done	8 2.4	25 7.4	49 14.5	168 49.6	89 26.3	3.90	0.952
SL21	Our manager treats honestly with people	6 1.8	22 6.5	37 10.9	175 51.6	99 29.2	4.00	0.907
SL22	Our manager encourages us to do the right thing	2 0.6	17 5.0	37 10.9	190 56	93 27.4	4.05	0.798
SL23	Our manager respects our views and takes our views into account	6 1.8	36 10.6	33 9.7	174 51.3	90 26.5	3.90	0.970
SL24	Our manager respects people's private life (privacy)	7 2.1	20 5.9	21 6.2	180 53.1	111 32.7	4.09	0.898
SL25	Our manager puts the interests of the organization ahead of his/her own interests	5 1.5	24 7.1	35 10.3	191 56.3	84 24.8	3.96	0.876

obtaining a factor as a result of grouping the variables that are related to each other and measure the same dimension by calculating the correlation between the variables according to the answers given by the respondents (Ural and Kılıç 2005).

When factor analysis is mentioned in social science research, two main types of analysis come to mind. These are exploratory factor analysis and confirmatory factor analysis (CFA). Exploratory factor analysis is mostly used to discover which factors constitute the variables observed in the early stages of a researcher's scale development studies. Besides, in CFA a large number of variables related to the considered concept (structure) are reduced or it is tried to discover less number of factors with higher explanatory power that explain this structure. Similarly, if it adds items to or removes items from the existing scales in the literature, it is considered that it would be appropriate to start the structural and factorial validity studies of the scale with CFA. Confirmatory factor analysis, on the other hand, is mostly preferred to confirm the accuracy of a scale or model that has been previously developed, used in previous studies, or has a solid theoretical basis, with the collected data.

Table 4.8 Descriptive statistics on the items of the organizational ambidexterity

Organizational ambidexterity		Strongly disagree	Disagree	Neither agree nor disagree	Agree	Strongly agree	Average	Standard deviation
		f_i f_i%	f_i f_i%	f_i f_i%	f_i f_i%	f_i f_i%	N = 339	
OAD1	Our company also responds to requests other than our current products and services	21 6.2	73 21.5	48 14.2	160 47.2	37 10.9	3.35	1.119
OAD2	Our company invents new products and services	7 2.1	32 9.4	43 12.7	167 49.3	90 26.5	3.89	0.973
OAD3	Our company tries new products and services in our local market	3 0.9	27 8.0	63 18.6	179 52.8	67 19.8	3.83	0.868
OAD4	In our company, our completely new products and services are commercialized	7 2.1	46 13.6	62 18.3	151 44.5	73 21.5	3.70	1.019
OAD5	Our company frequently evaluates new opportunities in new markets	4 1.2	28 8.3	58 17.1	170 50.1	79 23.3	3.86	0.908
OAD6	Our company uses new distribution channels regularly	10 2.9	71 20.9	74 21.8	128 37.8	56 16.5	3.44	1.084
OAD7	Our company seeks regularly new customers in new markets and strives to reach them	5 1.5	28 8.3	48 14.2	174 51.3	84 24.8	3.90	0.919
OAD8	Our company makes frequent improvements in the presentation of our existing products and services	1 0.3	44 13.0	52 15.3	173 51.0	69 20.4	3.78	0.926
OAD9	Our company regularly makes minor adaptations to our existing products and services	1 0.3	41 12.1	51 15.0	188 55.5	57 16.8	3,77	0,883
OAD10	Our company puts improved products and services on our local market	0 0.0	30 8.8	53 15.6	196 57.8	60 17.8	3,84	0,815
OAD11	Our company attaches importance to our supplies and improves the supply efficiency of our products and services	1 0.3	16 4.7	47 13.9	192 56.6	83 24.5	4.00	0.775
OAD12	Our company increases the economies of scale in existing markets	2 0.6	27 8.0	69 20.4	171 50.4	70 20.6	3.83	0.868

(continued)

Table 4.8 (continued)

Organizational ambidexterity		Strongly disagree	Disagree	Neither agree nor disagree	Agree	Strongly agree	Average	Standard deviation
		f_i $f_i\%$	f_i $f_i\%$	f_i $f_i\%$	f_i $f_i\%$	f_i $f_i\%$	N = 339	
OAD13	Our company expands its services for existing customers	1 0.3	12 3.5	33 9.7	205 60.5	88 26.0	4.08	0.721
OAD14	In our company, reducing the costs of internal processes is an important goal	0 0.0	7 2.1	33 9.7	172 50.7	127 37.5	4.24	0.707
OAD15	The management systems in our company work consistently to support all the goals of the company	0 0.0	15 4.4	50 14.7	177 52.2	97 28.6	4.05	0.781
OAD16	Company employees work in line with the same goals because our management systems avoid conflicting goals	1 0.3	27 8.0	49 14.5	197 58.1	65 19.2	3.88	0.818
OAD17	The management systems in our company prevent us from wasting resources with inefficient activities of employees	3 0.9	35 10.3	53 15.6	197 58.1	51 15.0	3.76	0.863
OAD18	The management systems in our company encourage employees to challenge outdated traditions / practices	5 1.5	45 13.3	60 17.7	179 52.8	50 14.7	3.66	0.936
OAD19	The management systems in our company are flexible enough to allow us to respond quickly to changes in the market	9 2.7	93 27.4	68 20.1	131 38.6	38 11.2	3.28	1.067
OAD20	Management systems in our company show rapid development in responding (response) to changes in our work priorities	12 3.5	87 25.7	79 23.3	123 36.3	38 11.2	3.26	1.070

In other words, if a researcher is using scales that were previously used and their factorial structures are known, it is stated that it would be more accurate to prefer CFA. Based on this understanding (Gürbüz 2019), which is becoming more and more widely accepted among social science researches, since the scales used in many scientific researches were used in our study, confirmatory factor analysis was performed without performing exploratory factor analysis. The analysis was made

Table 4.9 Descriptive statistics on the Items of the organizational agility

Organizational agility		Strongly disagree	Disagree	Neither agree nor disagree	Agree	Strongly agree	Average	Standard deviation
		f_i f_i%	f_i f_i%	f_i f_i%	f_i f_i%	f_i f_i%	N = 339	
AG1	Our company has got a strategic vision that will achieve its long-term goals	3 0.9	16 4.7	24 7.1	192 56.6	104 30.7	4.12	0.797
AG2	Our company has got adequate amount of and efficacious technology in accordance with the requirements of the age	1 0.3	15 4.4	38 11.2	164 48.4	121 35.7	4.15	0.808
AG3	Our company's product quality and as well as the service quality for this product is high	0 0.0	8 2.4	32 9.4	165 48.7	134 39.5	4.25	0.722
AG4	Our company aims to achieve the maximum output with the minimum input in all processes in order to achieve its goal	0 0.0	18 5.3	40 11.8	171 50.4	110 32.4	4.10	0.804
AG5	Our company makes high level product promotions	5 1.5	67 19.8	75 22.1	120 35.4	72 21.2	3.55	1.077
AG6	Our company has expert and authorized human resources	2 0.6	40 11.8	50 14.7	181 53.4	66 19.5	3.79	0.909
AG7	All business processes in our company are defined simply, loud and clearly	1 0.3	44 13.0	56 16.5	170 50.1	68 20.1	3.77	0.927
AG8	Our company attaches importance to provide and develop cooperation environment inside and outside the business	4 1.2	25 7.4	56 16.5	190 56.0	64 18.9	3.84	0.856

(continued)

Table 4.9 (continued)

Organizational agility		Strongly disagree	Disagree	Neither agree nor disagree	Agree	Strongly agree	Average	Standard deviation
		f_i f_i%	f_i f_i%	f_i f_i%	f_i f_i%	f_i f_i%	N = 339	
AG9	Our company has the efficiency of producing different product models	1 0.3	62 18.3	45 13.3	156 46.0	75 22.1	3.71	1.016
AG10	Our company has the flexibility of producing different amount of products and services	4 1.2	45 13.3	48 14.2	167 49.3	75 22.1	3.78	0.977
AG11	Our company has flexibility within the scope of human resources policies	6 1.8	56 16.5	62 18.3	171 50.4	44 13.0	3.56	0,972
AG12	Our company has the ability to respond quickly to changes in the customer's needs and preferences	1 0.3	26 7.7	61 18.0	197 58.1	54 15.9	3.82	0.801
AG13	Our company feels and perceives the direction of change within the scope of environmental change and holds itself in readiness for these changes	1 0.3	27 8.0	65 19.2	191 56.3	55 16.2	3.80	0.814
AG14	Our company's ability to adapt innovations and overcome the environmental and technology-induced changes quickly and timely is higher than its competitors	0 0.0	34 10.0	68 20.1	187 55.2	50 14.7	3.75	0.829
AG15	Our company is faster in production processes compared to its competitors	0 0.0	49 14.5	80 23.6	161 47.5	49 14.5	3.62	0.903
AG16	Our company is fast in introducing new products to the market	3 0.9	49 14.5	93 27.4	143 42.2	51 15.0	3.56	0.944

(continued)

Table 4.9 (continued)

Organizational agility		Strongly disagree	Disagree	Neither agree nor disagree	Agree	Strongly agree	Average	Standard deviation
		f_i $f_i\%$	f_i $f_i\%$	f_i $f_i\%$	f_i $f_i\%$	f_i $f_i\%$	N = 339	
AG17	Our company distributes products and services to the customers quickly and on time	1 0,3	24 7.1	56 16.5	182 53.7	76 22.4	3.91	0.832

Table 4.10 Reliability analysis results of the scales used in the study

Scales	Dimensions	Cronbach alpha (α) coefficients
Strategic leadership	MSL	0.677
	TSL	0.835
	PSL	0.798
	CSL	0.868
	ESL	0.840
Organizational agility	CMP	0.819
	FLX	0.636
	ANS	0.720
	SPD	0.747
Organizational ambidexterity	EXR	0.809
	EXV	0.774
	ABY	0.794
	ADT	0.712

with the AMOS 20 package program, and the degree of compliance of the data with the default model was tested.

The variables take place in the analyzes and the abbreviations used for their sub-dimensions are shown below.

Strategic leadership	(SL)
Managing	(MSL)
Transforming	(TSL)
Political	(PSL)
Communicational	(CSL)
Ethical	(ESL)
Organizational ambidexterity	*(OAD)*

(continued)

(continued)

Exploratory innovation	(EXR)
Exploitative innovation	(EXV)
Alignment	(ABY)
Adaptability	(ADT)
Organizational agility	*(AG)*
Competency	(CMP)
Flexibility	(FLX)
Responsiveness/answer	(ANS)
Quickness/speed	(SPD)

Confirmatory Factor Analysis (CFA) Regarding the Scales Used

In structural equation models, the conceptual model that exists in theory is tried to be tested with the help of data. Confirmatory factor analysis aims to determine the accuracy of a predetermined structure (Karagöz 2019). In this chapter, confirmatory factor analyzes applied to the scales we used in our research are included.

Confirmatory Factor Analysis of Strategic Leadership Scale

Confirmatory factor analysis was applied to the strategic leadership scale consisting of five dimensions, CFA path diagram (Fig. 4.11), CFA standardized regression coefficients (Table 4.11) and CFA fit values (Table 4.12) are shown in the figures and tables.

Looking at Fig. 4.11, standardized path coefficients between latent variables and observed variables are seen in the strategic leadership confirmatory factor analysis path diagram.

When Table 4.11 is examined, the fact that all of the P values of the bilateral relations between the variables are less than 0.05 indicates that the bilateral relations are statistically significant.

When the standardized regression coefficients (path coefficients) are reviewed, it is seen that, the standardized regression coefficients for the items predicting the transformational strategic leadership (TSL) latent variable varies between 0.6289 and 0.8150, the standardized regression coefficients for the items predicting the political strategic leadership (PSL) latent variable varies between 0.5317 and 0.7349, the standardized regression coefficients for the items predicting the communicational strategic leadership (CSL) latent variable varies between 0.6090 and 0.8682, the standardized regression coefficients for the items predicting the managerial strategic leadership (MSL) latent variable varies between 0.4024 and 0.7642, and the standardized regression coefficients for the items predicting the ethical strategic leadership (ESL) latent variable varies between 0.5939 and 0.8065.

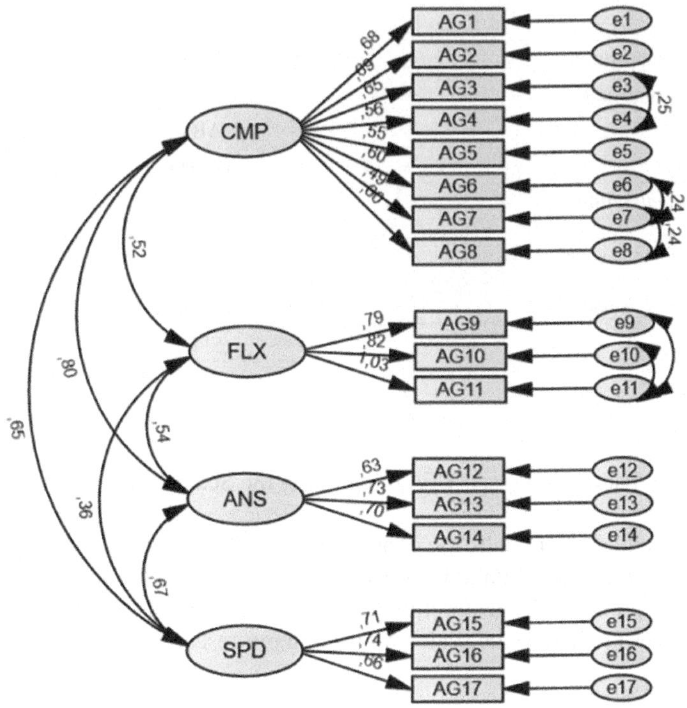

Fig. 4.11 Strategic leadership CFA path diagram

It is desirable that the factor loadings of the variables are ideally above 0.5 (Gürbüz 2019). It is seen that SL3, SL4 and SL5 have values very close to 0.5 and factor loads of all other variables are above 0.5. The model fit values of the model, which was determined to be statistically significant according to the estimation results, are shown in Table 4.12.

First-level Confirmatory Factor Analysis, consisting of five sub-dimensions and 25 items of the Strategic Leadership Scale, was tested. As a result of the performed Confirmatory Factor Analysis, correction indices were examined to obtain acceptable goodness of fit values. Thus, the proposed five-factor model was found to be compatible with the data and acceptable.

Confirmatory Factor Analysis of Organizational Ambidexterity Scale

Confirmatory factor analysis was applied to the organizational ambidexterity scale, CFA path diagram (Fig. 4.12.), CFA standardized regression coefficients (Table 4.13) and CFA fit values (Table 4.14) are shown in the figures and tables.

By creating a first level confirmatory factor analysis model, the latent variables in the structure of the organizational ambidexterity scale and the interdependent effects between these factors were tested. Latent variables are variables that cannot

Table 4.11 Significance levels of strategic leadership confirmatory factor analysis

Parameters			Standardized regression coefficients	P
SL10	←	TSL	0.6289	
SL9	←	TSL	0.8150	***
SL8	←	TSL	0.7054	***
SL7	←	TSL	0.7356	***
SL6	←	TSL	0.6677	***
SL15	←	PSL	0.7349	
SL14	←	PSL	0.5317	***
SL13	←	PSL	0.6843	***
SL12	←	PSL	0.6195	***
SL11	←	PSL	0.6246	***
SL20	←	CSL	0.8022	
SL19	←	CSL	0.8589	***
SL18	←	CSL	0.8682	***
SL17	←	CSL	0.6090	***
SL16	←	CSL	0.6492	***
SL5	←	MSL	0.4329	
SL4	←	MSL	0.4927	***
SL3	←	MSL	0.4024	***
SL2	←	MSL	0.7642	***
SL1	←	MSL	0.6440	***
SL25	←	ESL	0.5939	
SL24	←	ESL	0.6948	***
SL23	←	ESL	0.7385	***
SL22	←	ESL	0.7550	***
SL21	←	ESL	0.8065	***

be observed directly and explain a theoretical structure by associating it with scale items (Weston and Gore 2006). The CFA path diagram of the scale, which consists of four dimensions, is shown in Fig. 4.12.

In Table 4.13, it was understood that the bilateral relations were statistically significant because the P values were $p < 0.05$. When factor loadings are reviewed, it is seen that, the standardized regression coefficients for the items predicting the exploratory innovation (EXR) latent variable varies between 0.3660 and 0.7207, the standardized regression coefficients for the items predicting the exploitative innovation (EXV) latent variable varies between 0.3563 and 0.7476, the standardized regression coefficients for the items predicting the alignment (ABY) latent variable varies between 0.7167 and 0.8166, and the standardized regression coefficients for

Table 4.12 Confirmatory factor analysis fit values of the strategic leadership scale

Goodness of fit measures	Good fit	Acceptable fit	Calculated value	References
Chi-square fit test $\chi 2$ CMIN	Significant p value	–	540.2598	Yaşlıoğlu (2017)
General model fit $\chi 2/df$	≤ 3	≤ 4–5	2.062	Meydan and Şeşen (2015), Zhu et al. (2015), Wang et al. (2014)
Normed fit indices NFI	≥ 0.90	>0.80	0.864	Meydan and Şeşen (2015), Yaşlıoğlu (2017)
Incremental fit indices IFI	≥ 0.95	0.94–0.90	0.925	Meydan and Şeşen (2015), Wang et al. (2014)
Comparative fit indices CFI	≥ 0.97	≥ 0.90	0.924	Meydan and Şeşen (2015), Kanste et al. (2006), Yaşlıoğlu (2017), Wang et al. (2014)
Root mean square of approximate errors RMSEA	≤ 0.05	≤ 0.08	0.0561	Meydan and Şeşen (2015), Wang et al. (2014)
Goodness fit indices GFI	≥ 0.90	0.89–0.85	0.891	Meydan and Şeşen (2015)
Adjusted goodness fit indices AGFI	≥ 0.90	≥ 0.80	0.865	Meydan and Şeşen (2015), Kanste et al. (2006)
Parsimony normed compliance indices—parsimony goodness fit indices PNFI-PGFI	≥ 0.95–≥ 0.95	>0.5–>0.5	0.754	Meydan and Şeşen (2015), Fu and Deshpande (2014)
Square root of mean errors RMR	≤ 0.05	Moderate fit 0.06–0.10 Weak fit ≥ 0.10	0.057	Meydan and Şeşen 92015), Politis (2004)
Standardized RMR	<0.05	≤ 0.08	0.0647	Gürbüz (2019)

the items predicting the adaptability (ADT) latent variable varies between 0.3605 and 0.8951.

First-level Confirmatory Factor Analysis, consisting of four sub-dimensions and 20 items of the Organizational Ambidexterity Scale, was tested. As a result of the performed Confirmatory Factor Analysis, correction indices were examined to obtain acceptable goodness of fit values. Thus, the proposed four-factor model was found to be compatible with the data and acceptable.

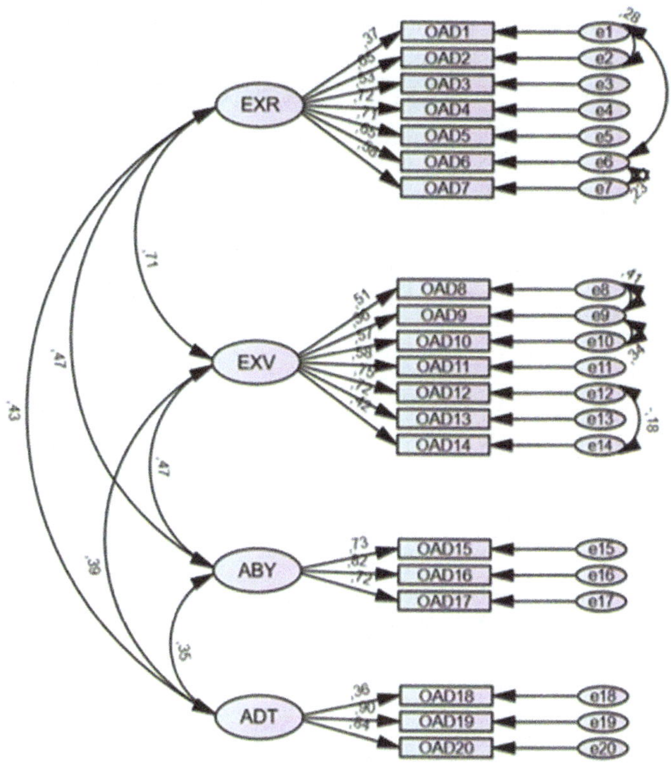

Fig. 4.12 Organizational ambidexterity CFA path diagram

Confirmatory Factor Analysis of the Organizational Agility Scale

The organizational agility scale, which consists of competence, flexibility, responsiveness and speed dimensions, was evaluated with the first level CFA. The predictive power between the parameters in the structure of the organizational agility scale and the latent factors was tested by creating a first-level CFA model. Organizational agility scale CFA path diagram is shown in Fig. 4.13.

Since the p values in the organizational agility scale were $p < 0.05$, it was found to be statistically significant (Table 4.15). When factor loadings are reviewed, it is seen that, the standardized regression coefficients for the items predicting competency (CMP) latent variable varies between 0.486 and 0.693, the standardized regression coefficients for the items predicting flexibility (FLX) latent variable varies between 0.894 and 1.027, the standardized regression coefficients for the items predicting responsiveness (ANS) latent variable varies between 0.626 and 0.731, and the standardized regression coefficients for the items predicting quickness (SPD) latent variable varies between 0.665 and 0.739 (Table 4.15).

First-level Confirmatory Factor Analysis, consisting of four sub-dimensions and 17 items of the Organizational Agility Scale, was tested. As a result of the performed

Table 4.13 Significance levels of confirmatory factor analysis related to organizational ambidexterity scale

Parameters			Standardized regression coefficients	P
OAD1	←	EXR	0.3660	
OAD2	←	EXR	0.6491	***
OAD3	←	EXR	0.5328	***
OAD4	←	EXR	0.7207	***
OAD5	←	EXR	0.7147	***
OAD6	←	EXR	0.6477	***
OAD7	←	EXR	0.5764	***
OAD8	←	EXV	0.5132	
OAD9	←	EXV	0.3563	***
OAD10	←	EXV	0.5738	***
OAD11	←	EXV	0.5838	***
OAD12	←	EXV	0.7476	***
OAD13	←	EXV	0.7229	***
OAD14	←	EXV	0.4188	***
OAD15	←	ABY	0.7258	
OAD16	←	ABY	0.8166	***
OAD17	←	ABY	0.7167	***
OAD18	←	ADT	0.3605	
OAD19	←	ADT	0.8951	***
OAD20	←	ADT	0.8358	***

Confirmatory Factor Analysis, correction indices were examined to obtain acceptable goodness of fit values. Thus, the proposed four-factor model was found to be compatible with the data and acceptable (Table 4.16).

4.8.3 Testing the Research Model

It was postulated that the factors (latent variables) in the research model; managerial strategic leadership (MSL), transformational strategic leadership (TSL), political strategic leadership (PSL), communicative strategic leadership (CSL), ethical strategic leadership (ESL) exploratory innovation (EXR), exploitative innovation (EXV), alignment (ABY), adaptability (ADT) and competency (CMP), flexibility (FLX), responsiveness (ANS), and quickness (SPD) and also the causal relationships between these factors can be explained. In the research model, strategic leadership (SL), organizational ambidexterity (OAD) and organizational agility (AG) factors

Table 4.14 Confirmatory factor analysis fit values of the organizational ambidexterity scale

Goodness of fit measures	Good fit	Acceptable fit	Calculated value	References
Chi-square fit test $\chi 2$ CMIN	Significant p value	–	496.11	Yaşlıoğlu (2017)
General model fit $\chi 2/df$	≤3	≤4–5	3.14	Meydan and Şeşen (2015), Zhu et al. (2015), Wang et al. (2014)
Normed fit indices NFI	≥0.90	>0.80	0.812	Meydan and Şeşen (2015), Yaşlıoğlu (2017)
Incremental fit indices IFI	≥0.95	0.94–0.90	0.864	Meydan and Şeşen (2015), Wang et al. (2014)
Comparative fit indices CFI	≥0.97	≥0.90	0.862	Meydan and Şeşen (2015), Kanste et al. (2006), Yaşlıoğlu (2017), Wang et al. (2014)
Root mean square of approximate errors RMSEA	≤0.05	≤0.08	0.079	Meydan and Şeşen (2015), Wang et al. (2014)
Goodness fit indices GFI	≥0.90	0.89–0.85	0.872	Meydan and Şeşen (2015)
Adjusted goodness fit indices AGFI	≥0.90	≥0.80	0.829	Meydan and Şeşen (2015), Kanste et al. (2006)
Parsimony normed compliance indices—parsimony goodness fit indices PNFI-PGFI	≥0.95–≥0.95	>0.5–>0.5	0.675	Meydan and Şeşen (2015), Fu and Deshpande (2014)
Square root of mean errors RMR	≤0.05	Moderate fit 0.06–0.10 Weak fit ≥0.10	0.067	Meydan and Şeşen (2015), Politis (2004)
Standardized RMR	<0.05	≤0.08	0.0852	Gürbüz (2019)

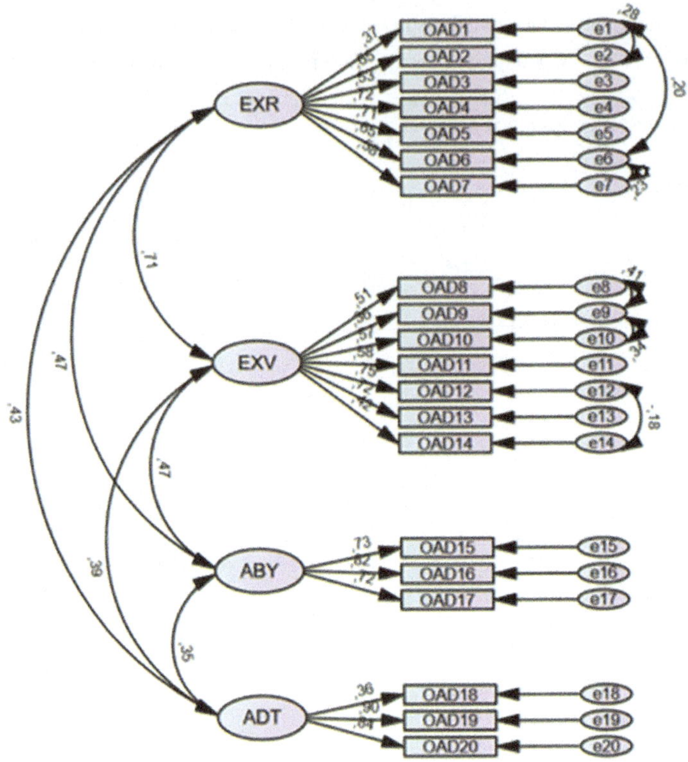

Fig. 4.13 Organizational agility CFA path diagram

were not considered one-dimensional, and assuming that they were explained by the latent variables of each, the model in Fig. 4.14 was created.

It was determined that the data could not provide the multivariate normal assumption from the SEM assumptions. Byrne (2010) stated that especially in studies in which Likert type scales were used, the concentration of participants on the same item caused the distribution to deviate from the normal. On the other hand, bootstrap method is recommended as an auxiliary method for data that cannot provide the normality assumption. In the analysis of our study, the bootstrap method was used.

In the structural equation model analysis, direct and indirect causality analysis between variables can be tested. Accordingly, in our study, while direct causality between strategic leadership scale sub-dimensions and organizational ambidexterity sub-dimensions and between strategic leadership sub-dimensions and organizational agility sub-dimensions were investigated, at the same time, an indirect or mediator effect can be tested between the sub-dimensions of organizational ambidexterity by means of the sub-dimensions of the strategic leadership scale and the sub-dimensions of organizational agility.

Table 4.15 Significance levels of confirmatory factor analysis related to organizational agility scale

Parameters			Standardized regression coefficients	P
AG1	←	CMP	0.6826	
AG2	←	CMP	0.6931	***
AG3	←	CMP	0.6523	***
AG4	←	CMP	0.5620	***
AG5	←	CMP	0.5462	***
AG6	←	CMP	0.5970	***
AG7	←	CMP	0.4858	***
AG8	←	CMP	0.5957	***
AG9	←	FLX	0.7935	
AG10	←	FLX	0.8171	***
AG11	←	FLX	1.0272	***
AG12	←	ANS	0.6261	
AG13	←	ANS	0.7309	***
AG14	←	ANS	0.6971	***
AG15	←	SPD	0.7106	
AG16	←	SPD	0.7390	***
AG17	←	SPD	0.6648	***

When the model in Fig. 4.14 was tested, the presence of statistically insignificant paths was detected and it was understood that they should be removed from the model. Since the significance levels of the relationships will interact, the non-significant paths were not removed from the model at one, but one by one, and the analysis was repeated, and the model was re-estimated as in Fig. 4.15.

Statistical significance of the regression coefficients was tested in Table 4.17 and it was determined that all parameters were significant.

As seen in Table 4.18, while 0.32 of the changes in adaptation ability (ADT) from organizational ambidexterity sub-dimensions were explained, 0.43 of changes in adaptability (ADL), 0.68 of exploitative innovation ability (EXV), 0.68 of exploratory innovation ability (EXR) 0.7436 were explained. From organizational agility sub-dimensions, 0.8058 of competence (CMP), 0.4405 of flexibility (FLX), 0.4406 of quickness (SPD), and 0.7697 of responsiveness (ANS) are explained.

In line with the hypotheses of the research model, the verification of the measurement model consisting of the sub-dimensions of the Strategic Leadership scale, MSL, TSL, PSL, CSL and ESL, the sub-dimensions EXR, EXV, ABY and ADT of the Organizational Ambidexterity, and the sub-dimensions CMP, FLX, ANS and SPD of Organizational Agility, were tested with the assistance of AMOS package program. Goodness of fit indices in the analysis results are at acceptable values.

Based on the results of the analysis, the statistically significant parameters of the variables, which are the sub-dimensions of the scales, are given in Table 4.17.

Table 4.16 Confirmatory factor analysis fit values of organizational agility scale

Goodness of fit measures	Good fit	Acceptable fit	Calculated value	References
Chi-square fit test $\chi 2$ CMIN	Significant p value	–	276.11	Yaşlıoğlu (2017)
General model fit $\chi 2/df$	≤ 3	$\leq 4–5$	2.55	Meydan and Şeşen (2015), Zhu et al. (2015), Wang et al. (2014)
Normed fit indices NFI	≥ 0.90	>0.80	0.871	Meydan and Şeşen (2015), Yaşlıoğlu (2017)
Incremental fit indices IFI	≥ 0.95	0.94–0.90	0.917	Meydan and Şeşen (2015), Wang et al. (2014)
Comparative fit indices CFI	≥ 0.97	≥ 0.90	0.916	Meydan and Şeşen (2015), Kanste et al. (2006), Yaşlıoğlu (2017), Wang et al. (2014)
Root mean square of approximate errors RMSEA	≤ 0.05	≤ 0.08	0.067	Meydan and Şeşen (2015), Wang et al. (2014)
Goodness fit indices GFI	≥ 0.90	0.89–0.85	0.916	Meydan and Şeşen (2015)
Adjusted goodness fit indices AGFI	≥ 0.90	≥ 0.80	0.876	Meydan and Şeşen (2015), Kanste et al. (2006)
Parsimony normed compliance indices—parsimony goodness fit indices PNFI-PGFI	$\geq 0.95–\geq 0.95$	>0.5–>0.5	0.692	Meydan and Şeşen (2015), Fu and Deshpande (2014)
Square root of mean errors RMR	≤ 0.05	Moderate fit 0.06–0.10 Weak fit ≥ 0.10	0.040	Meydan and Şeşen (2015), Politis (2004)
Standardized RMR	<0.05	≤ 0.08	0.0510	Gürbüz (2019)

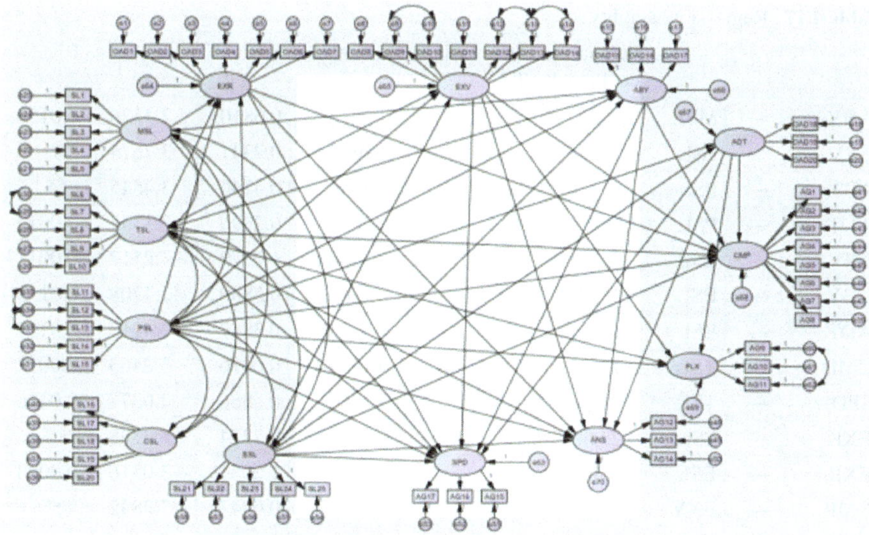

Fig. 4.14 Research model

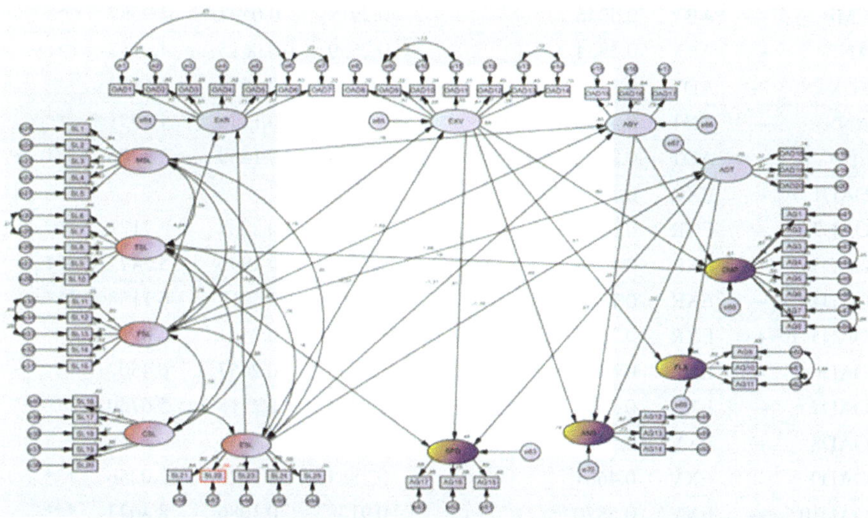

Fig. 4.15 Structural equation model

When one of the hypotheses (H2) of our research, that is the direct effect between the sub-dimensions of the strategic leadership scale and the sub-dimensions of Organizational Ambidexterity is tested; while MSL, which is the sub-dimension of Strategic Leadership, directly affects only the ARF dimension positively among the sub-dimensions of Organizational Ambidexterity, based on the test results it was

Table 4.17 Regression weights

			Standardized regression coefficients (β)	Estimate	S.E	C.R	P
ABY	←	MSL	0.1606	0.1972	0.0810	2.4326	0.0150
EXV	←	PSL	3.7778	2.7657	0.7341	3.7674	***
ABY	←	PSL	1.8247	1.4646	0.4240	3.4545	***
ADT	←	PSL	1.8622	0.9060	0.2890	3.1347	0.0017
EXV	←	ESL	−3.3092	−3.3420	1.0279	−3.2512	0.0011
ABY	←	ESL	−1.3122	−1.4530	0.5880	−2.4708	0.0135
ADT	←	ESL	−1.3862	−0.9304	0.3857	−2.4119	0.0159
CMP	←	TSL	0.1831	0.1999	0.0616	3.2463	0.0012
SPD	←	TSL	0.1429	0.1765	0.0866	2.0377	0.0416
EXR	←	PSL	4.2444	2.4577	0.7274	3.3788	***
EXR	←	ESL	−3.8321	-3.0611	1.0031	−3.0516	0.0023
CMP	←	EXV	0.5956	0.6257	0.0847	7.3842	***
FLX	←	EXV	0.5085	0.8126	0.1157	7.0258	***
ANS	←	EXV	0.4820	0.4920	0.0827	5.9508	***
SPD	←	EXV	0.4109	0.4881	0.0983	4.9644	***
CMP	←	ABY	0.3046	0.2919	0.0591	4.9387	***
ANS	←	ABY	0.2824	0.2629	0.0615	4.2757	***
FLX	←	ADT	0.2597	0.6244	0.1511	4.1323	***
ANS	←	ADT	0.3213	0.4935	0.1176	4.1951	***
SPD	←	ADT	0.2678	0.4788	0.1430	3.3476	***
OAD1	←	EXR	0.3706	1.0000			
OAD2	←	EXR	0.6496	1.5237	0.2268	6.7179	***
OAD3	←	EXR	0.5288	1.1071	0.1996	5.5472	***
OAD4	←	EXR	0.7243	1.7808	0.2912	6.1158	***
OAD5	←	EXR	0.7127	1.5601	0.2561	6.0924	***
OAD6	←	EXR	0.6549	1.7139	0.2657	6.4507	***
OAD7	←	EXR	0.5680	1.2585	0.2218	5.6750	***
OAD8	←	EXV	0.5662	1.0000			
OAD9	←	EXV	0.4661	0.7884	0.1122	7.0256	***
OAD10	←	EXV	0.5870	0.9128	0.1086	8.4023	***
OAD11	←	EXV	0.5530	0.8174	0.1015	8.0523	***
OAD12	←	EXV	0.6727	1.1138	0.1209	9.2153	***
OAD13	←	EXV	0.6710	0.9227	0.1004	9.1937	***
OAD14	←	EXV	0.3871	0.5222	0.0865	6.0375	***
OAD15	←	ABY	0.7360	1.0000			

(continued)

Table 4.17 (continued)

			Standardized regression coefficients (β)	Estimate	S.E	C.R	P
OAD16	←	ABY	0.7995	1.1374	0.0895	12.7058	***
OAD17	←	ABY	0.7203	1.0812	0.0915	11.8123	***
OAD18	←	ADT	0.3723	1.0000			
OAD19	←	ADT	0.8664	2.6531	0.4027	6.5886	***
OAD20	←	ADT	0.8566	2.6311	0.3995	6.5857	***

Table 4.18 Squared R^2 multiple correlations

	Estimate
ADT	0.3217
ABY	0.4281
EXV	0.6806
FLX	0.4405
SPD	0.4406
ANS	0.7436
CMP	0.8058
EXR	0.7697
OAD6	0.4289
OAD5	0.5080
OAD4	0.5247
OAD3	0.2797
OAD2	0.4220
OAD1	0.1373

determined that, it has no effect on the other sub-dimensions (EXR, EXV, ADT) of the Organizational Ambidexterity scale. Similarly, it was determined as a result of the test that TSL and CSL, which are the sub-dimensions of Strategic Leadership, have no direct effect on any of the sub-dimensions of Organizational Ambidexterity. Besides, PSL, which is also the sub-dimension of Strategic Leadership, directly affects all of the Organizational Ambidexterity sub-dimensions (EXR, EXV, ABY and ADT) in a positive way. In addition, it has been observed that the Strategic Leadership sub-dimension, ESL, has a direct negative effect on all sub-dimensions (EXR, EXV, ABY and ADT) of Organizational Ambidexterity.

When one of the hypotheses of H1, that is the direct effect between the sub-dimensions of the strategic leadership scale and the sub-dimensions of the Organizational Agility is tested, while MSL, TSL, CSL and ESL, which are the sub-dimensions of Strategic Leadership, do not directly affect any of the Organizational Agility sub-dimensions, as the result of the test it has been determined that, they directly affect

PSL that is the sub-dimension of Strategic Leadership and the CMP and SPD that are the sub-dimensions of Organizational Agility.

When one of the hypotheses of H3, which is the direct effect between the sub-dimensions of Organizational Ambidexterity and the sub-dimensions of strategic agility was tested, EXV which is one of the sub-dimensions of organizational ambidexterity is affecting positively all of the sub-dimensions (CMP, FLX, ANS and SPD) of organizational agility. Direct and indirect effects are given in Tables 4.19, 4.20, 4.21 and 4.22.

The relationship between the sub-dimensions of the strategic leadership scale and the Organizational Agility scale was tested whether the sub-dimensions of the Organizational Ambidexterity Scale had a mediating role. By increasing the number of observations to 10,000 by taking into account the Bootstrap method, on one hand it is aimed to bring the distribution of the data closer to normal, on the other hand, it has been tested whether the 95% confidence interval values of the indirect and mediating effects obtained in Table FF are valid. In the mediation effect analyzes made with the bootstrap technique, the values in the 95% confidence interval obtained as a result of the analysis should not include the "0" (zero) value in order to support the research hypotheses (Gürbüz 2019). Considering the values in Tables 4.23 and 4.24, it is seen that it does not include the value "0" (zero).

In our study, it was evaluated whether the effect of the strategic leadership independent variable on the organizational agility dependent variable was mediated by the organizational ambidexterity independent variable (indirect effect). As seen in Tables 4.23 and 4.24, it was determined by the test results that, the positive effect of political strategic leadership (PSL) dimension, which is one of the strategic leadership sub-dimensions on the organizational agility dimensions of flexibility (FLX), speed (SPD), quick response/responsiveness (ANS) and competence/competency (CMP) through organizational ambidexterity scale sub-dimensions is significant.

Besides this, it was also determined by the test results that, the negative effect of ethical strategic leadership (ESL) dimension, which is one of the strategic leadership sub-dimensions on the organizational agility dimensions of FLX, SPD, ANS and CMP through organizational ambidexterity scale sub-dimensions is significant.

In addition, it was determined that, the positive effect of MSL Dimension which is one of the strategic leadership sub-dimensions on the organizational agility dimensions of ANS and CMP through organizational ambidexterity scale sub-dimensions is significant.

When the analysis results of the data obtained from our research are evaluated; Among the research hypotheses given in Table 4.25, the "**SUPPORTED**" hypotheses are given in Table 4.25.

4.9 Discussion

While the results of our research are being evaluated, it should not be ignored that the study was conducted during the Covid-19 pandemic period. In fact, it is seen that,

Table 4.19 Standardized direct effects

	ESL	CSL	PSL	TSL	MSL	ADT	ABY	EXV	FLX	SPD	ANS	CMP	EXR
ADT	−1.3862	0.0000	1.8622	0.0000	0.0000	0.0000	0.0000	0.0000	0.0000	0.0000	0.0000	0.0000	0.0000
ABY	−1.3122	0.0000	1.8247	0.0000	0.1606	0.0000	0.0000	0.0000	0.0000	0.0000	0.0000	0.0000	0.0000
EXV	−3.3092	0.0000	3.7778	0.0000	0.0000	0.0000	0.0000	0.0000	0.0000	0.0000	0.0000	0.0000	0.0000
FLX	*0.0000*	0.0000	0.0000	0.0000	0.0000	0.2597	0.0000	0.5085	0.0000	0.0000	0.0000	0.0000	0.0000
SPD	0.0000	0.0000	0.0000	0.1429	0.0000	0.2678	0.0000	0.4109	0.0000	0.0000	0.0000	0.0000	0.0000
ANS	0.0000	0.0000	0.0000	0.0000	0.0000	0.3213	0.2824	0.4820	0.0000	0.0000	0.0000	0.0000	0.0000
CMP	0.0000	0.0000	0.0000	0.1831	0.0000	0.0000	0.3046	0.5956	0.0000	0.0000	0.0000	0.0000	0.0000
EXR	−3.8321	0.0000	4.2444	0.0000	0.0000	0.0000	0.0000	0.0000	0.0000	0.0000	0.0000	0.0000	0.0000

Table 4.20 Fit values of structural equation model

Goodness of fit measures	Good fit	Acceptable fit	Calculated value	References
Chi-square fit test χ2 CMIN	Significant p value	–	3425.92	Yaşlıoğlu (2017)
General model fit χ2/df	≤3	≤4–5	1.919	Meydan and Şeşen (2015), Zhu et al. (2015), Wang et al. (2014)
Normed fit indices NFI	≥0.90	>0.80	0.871	Meydan and Şeşen (2015), Yaşlıoğlu (2017)
Incremental fit indices IFI	≥0.95	0.94–0.90	0.827	Meydan and Şeşen (2015), Wang et al. (2014)
Comparative fit indices CFI	≥0.97	≥0.90	0.825	Meydan and Şeşen (2015), Kanste et al. (2006), Yaşlıoğlu (2017), Wang et al. (2014)
Root mean square of approximate errors RMSEA	≤0.05	≤0.08	0.067	Meydan and Şeşen (2015), Wang et al. (2014)
Goodness fit indices GFI	≥0.90	0.89–0.85	0.748	Meydan and Şeşen (2015)
Adjusted goodness fit indices AGFI	≥0.90	≥0.80	0.725	Meydan and Şeşen (2015), Kanste et al. (2006)
Parsimony normed compliance indices—parsimony goodness fit indices PNFI-PGFI	≥0.95–≥0.95	>0.5–>0.5	0.657	Meydan and Şeşen (2015), Fu and Deshpande (2014)
Square root of mean errors RMR	≤0.05	Moderate fit 0.06–0.10 Weak fit ≥0.10	0.060	Meydan and Şeşen (2015), Politis (2004)

Table 4.21 Standardized indirect effects

	ESL	CSL	PSL	TSL	MSL	ADT	ABY	EXV	FLX	SPD	ANS	CMP	EXR
ADT	0.0000	0.0000	0.0000	0.0000	0.0000	0.0000	0.0000	0.0000	0.0000	0.0000	0.0000	0.0000	0.0000
ABY	0.0000	0.0000	0.0000	0.0000	0.0000	0.0000	0.0000	0.0000	0.0000	0.0000	0.0000	0.0000	0.0000
EXV	0.0000	0.0000	0.0000	0.0000	0.0000	0.0000	0.0000	0.0000	0.0000	0.0000	0.0000	0.0000	0.0000
FLX	−2.0427	0.0000	2.4047	0.0000	0.0000	0.0000	0.0000	0.0000	0.0000	0.0000	0.0000	0.0000	0.0000
SPD	−1.7308	0.0000	2.0509	0.0000	0.0000	0.0000	0.0000	0.0000	0.0000	0.0000	0.0000	0.0000	0.0000
ANS	−2.4112	0.0000	2.9348	0.0000	0.0454	0.0000	0.0000	0.0000	0.0000	0.0000	0.0000	0.0000	0.0000
CMP	−2.3708	0.0000	2.8061	0.0000	0.0489	0.0000	0.0000	0.0000	0.0000	0.0000	0.0000	0.0000	0.0000
EXR	0.0000	0.0000	0.0000	0.0000	0.0000	0.0000	0.0000	0.0000	0.0000	0.0000	0.0000	0.0000	0.0000

Table 4.22 Standardized indirect effects

	ESL	CSL	PSL	TSL	MSL
ADT	0.000	0.000	0.000	0.000	0.000
ABY	0.000	0.000	0.000	0.000	0.000
EXV	0.000	0.000	0.000	0.000	0.000
FLX	−2.041	0.000	2.402	0.000	0.000
SPD	−1.708	0.000	2.025	0.000	0.000
ANS	−2.549	0.000	3.110	0.000	0.049
CMP	−2.365	0.000	2.800	0.000	0.049
EXR	0.000	0.000	0.000	0.000	0.000

such an extraordinary situation has led to an important continuum for organizations to test themselves and see their true existence, skills and power. In this continuum, the strong organizations survived and some of them even got stronger; the ones who have shortcomings struggled to survive, and the weak ones unfortunately had to end their activities. For example, when we review the 500 Top Industrial Enterprises Lists announced every year by the Istanbul Chamber of Industry and make a comparison between 2019 and 2020, we see that 221 companies have rallied in 2020, 190 companies have decreased, 13 companies have kept their rank, 55 companies have just entered the list, and 68 companies were not included in the list.

It is important for organizations to achieve sustainable success and growth, not only to survive in extraordinary situations but in normalcy as well, provide a competitive advantage and to maintain this competitive advantage. In fact, considering the rapid developments in today's communication and information technologies, it is seen how cruel the conditions of competition are.

For organizations to be able to come through from such processes successfully, they need to be agile. Agility can be achieved with an organization and workforce having *competencies*, being *flexible*, *responding* instantly to needs and changing market conditions, and acting quickly (*quickness*).

In order to achieve these, organizations should make the best use of the assets in their structure (*exploitative innovation ability*), should be able to make innovations required by the challenging conditions they face (*exploratory innovation ability*) rapidly, for this, they should perform a harmonious work (*alignment*) between all business units, and they should have the ability to restructure (*adaptability*) their activities according to changing consumer needs (*ambidexterity*). On the other hand, to have an ambidextrous strategic leader or leaders who have the cultural background and knowledge to carry out all these activities and administrations, who know what kind of applications they can do under which conditions, who think strategically and who have strategic management skills are all important for success.

We name this "Organizational Mastery", having all these skills, assets and competencies we mentioned and being successful in changing and unpredictable conditions by performing these practices together. Although there are some studies that refer

Table 4.23 Indirect effects—lower bounds

	ESL	CSL	PSL	TSL	MSL	ADT	ABY	EXV	FLX	SPD	ANS	CMP	EXR
ADT	0.000	0.000	0.000	0.000	0.000	0.000	0.000	0.000	0.000	0.000	0.000	0.000	0.000
ABY	0.000	0.000	0.000	0.000	0.000	0.000	0.000	0.000	0.000	0.000	0.000	0.000	0.000
EXV	0.000	0.000	0.000	0.000	0.000	0.000	0.000	0.000	0.000	0.000	0.000	0.000	0.000
FLX	−7.422	0.000	1.799	0.000	0.000	0.000	0.000	0.000	0.000	0.000	0.000	0.000	0.000
SPD	−4.786	0.000	1.058	0.000	0.000	0.000	0.000	0.000	0.000	0.000	0.000	0.000	0.000
ANS	−6.229	0.000	1.336	0.000	0.016	0.000	0.000	0.000	0.000	0.000	0.000	0.000	0.000
CMP	−5.741	0.000	1.317	0.000	0.018	0.000	0.000	0.000	0.000	0.000	0.000	0.000	0.000
EXR	0.000	0.000	0.000	0.000	0.000	0.000	0.000	0.000	0.000	0.000	0.000	0.000	0.000

Table 4.24 Indirect effects—upper bounds

	ESL	CSL	PSL	TSL	MSL	ADT	ABY	EXV	FLX	SPD	ANS	CMP	EXR
ADT	0.000	0.000	0.000	0.000	0.000	0.000	0.000	0.000	0.000	0.000	0.000	0.000	0.000
ABY	0.000	0.000	0.000	0.000	0.000	0.000	0.000	0.000	0.000	0.000	0.000	0.000	0.000
EXV	0.000	0.000	0.000	0.000	0.000	0.000	0.000	0.000	0.000	0.000	0.000	0.000	0.000
FLX	−1.855	0.000	5.762	0.000	0.000	0.000	0.000	0.000	0.000	0.000	0.000	0.000	0.000
SPD	−1.093	0.000	3.769	0.000	0.000	0.000	0.000	0.000	0.000	0.000	0.000	0.000	0.000
ANS	−1.294	0.000	4.808	0.000	0.116	0.000	0.000	0.000	0.000	0.000	0.000	0.000	0.000
CMP	−1.347	0.000	4.514	0.000	0.129	0.000	0.000	0.000	0.000	0.000	0.000	0.000	0.000
EXR	0.000	0.000	0.000	0.000	0.000	0.000	0.000	0.000	0.000	0.000	0.000	0.000	0.000

Table 4.25 Supported hypotheses according to analysis results

H1	*Strategic leadership has a positive effect on organizational agility*
H1ba	Transformative leadership has a positive effect on competence
H1bd	Transformative leadership has a positive effect on speed
H2	*Strategic leadership has a positive effect on organizational ambidexterity*
H2ac	Managerial strategic leadership has a positive effect on alignment ability
H2ca	Political strategic leadership has a positive effect on explorative innovation ambidexterity
H2cb	Political strategic leadership has a positive effect on exploitative innovation ambidexterity
H2cc	Political strategic leadership has a positive effect on alignment ability
H2cd	Political strategic leadership has a positive effect on adaptability
H3	*Organizational ambidexterity has a positive effect on organizational agility*
H3ba	Exploitative innovation ambidexterity has a positive effect on competency
H3bb	Exploitative innovation ambidexterity has a positive effect on flexibility
H3bc	Exploitative innovation ambidexterity has a positive effect on responsiveness
H3ca	Alignment has a positive effect on competency
H3cc	Alignment has a positive effect on responsiveness
H3db	Adaptability has a positive effect on flexibility
H3dc	Adaptability has a positive effect on responsiveness
H3dd	Adaptability has a positive effect on speed
H4	*Organizational ambidexterity has a mediating role in the relationship between strategic leadership and organizational agility*
H4aa	Organizational ambidexterity has a mediating role in the relationship between managerial strategic leadership and competency
H4ac	Organizational ambidexterity has a mediating role in the relationship between managerial strategic leadership and responsiveness
H4ca	Organizational ambidexterity has a mediating role in the relationship between political strategic leadership and competency
H4cb	Organizational ambidexterity has a mediating role in the relationship between political strategic leadership and flexibility
H4cc	Organizational ambidexterity has a mediating role in the relationship between political strategic leadership and responsiveness
H4cd	Organizational ambidexterity has a mediating role in the relationship between political strategic leadership and speed

to the organizational ambidexterity as "Organizational Mastery", we take it one step further and expand the content of this concept a little more. Our study was carried out in order to reveal whether the effect of strategic leadership on the agility of organizations is directly or through organizational ambidexterity. Below, some studies on these variables in the literature (there are not many studies dealing with the dimensions of research variables in the literature) are given and these studies will be compared with the results we obtained from our study.

Crocitto and Youssef (2003) consider that adaptive organizations move from economies of scale to economies of scope, which is achieved by being agile in the market, and states that agility depends on the leadership's ability to create an agile vision and mission.

According to the transformational leadership theory of James Mac Gregor Burns (1978), which has an important place among the studies on leadership, transformational leadership comes to fruition when leaders establish relationships with their followers in a way that raises each other to higher levels of motivation and morality. At the same time, in the transformational leadership even though the goals of the leaders and their followers are different but related at the beginning, later they merge (Mulla and Krishnan 2009). Starting from this point of view, it is possible to say that transformational leadership behaviors can be effective in influencing the goals of followers, increasing their competencies and work performance, and this may be effective in organizational agility.

Veisch et al. (2014), in their studies, demonstrated that the transformational leadership style is effective on organizational agility and mentioned about the importance of organizational agility in increasing organizational performance in today's competitive environment. In the study of Wanasida et al. (2021), suggest that there is a direct positive relationship between transformational leadership and stated that organizational agility, and the greater the transformational leadership, the more positive its effect on organizational agility is seen. In our study, a result compatible with the literature was obtained; it was seen that the transformational leadership, which we consider as a dimension of strategic leadership, directly and positively affects the competence and speed dimensions of organizational agility, and the hypotheses (H1ba and H1bd) were supported as well (Fig. 4.16).

In the study of Çekmecelioğlu et al. (2018); the effect of transformational leadership behaviors on employees' displaying both exploratory and developmental behaviors simultaneously was revealed, and results were obtained to support that transformational leadership is an important antecedent in terms of ambidexterity. In our study, no effect of transformational strategic leadership on organizational ambidexterity was detected. Thus, the relevant hypotheses were rejected.

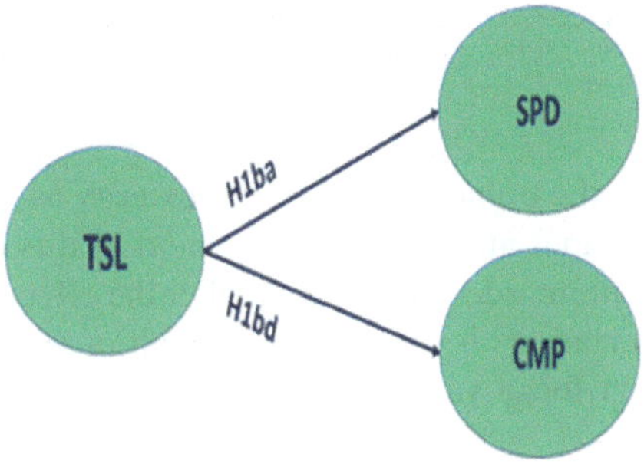

Fig. 4.16 The effect of transformational leadership on organizational agility dimensions

In our study, it was seen that three dimensions of organizational ambidexterity had a direct and positive effect on different dimensions of organizational agility. The exploitative innovation capability has a positive effect on competence (H3ba), flexibility (H3bb), responsiveness (H3bc) and speed (H3bd) among organizational agility dimensions. It was determined that the ability of adaptation has a direct and positive effect on competence (H3ca), responsiveness (H3cc), and adaptability has a direct and positive effect on flexibility (H3db), responsiveness (H3dc) and speed (H3dd). Thus, all the nine hypotheses were accepted and the results are consistent with the results of the studies in the literature. Some studies are as follows. For example, Zhou et al. (2018), in their research, concluded that operational-level informational systems alignment ambidexterity positively affects organizational agility (Fig. 4.17).

Clauβ et al. (2020), in their study on 150 medium-sized companies, purported how ambidexterity, exploration and exploitation together with strategic agility affect the competitive advantage of companies, they suggested that in order to remain competitive, companies should either choose the exploration strategy to be able to produce new information, products and services, or combine the exploitation strategy with strategic agility. Lee et al. (2015) stated that IT versatility improves organizational agility by facilitating operational versatility.

The change in customer demands and the increase in competition between enterprises to meet the personal demands of customers also change the conditions of competition. Responding to expected or unexpected changes in technology, communication, market and many areas accurately and on time, adapting to conditions and even being proactive are more important in this new economy structure for businesses. It is understood that, the participants think that exploitative, adaptation and adaptability efforts will make their companies more agile than innovation activities. It is seen that both structural and contextual ambidexterity affect organizational agility at the same time.

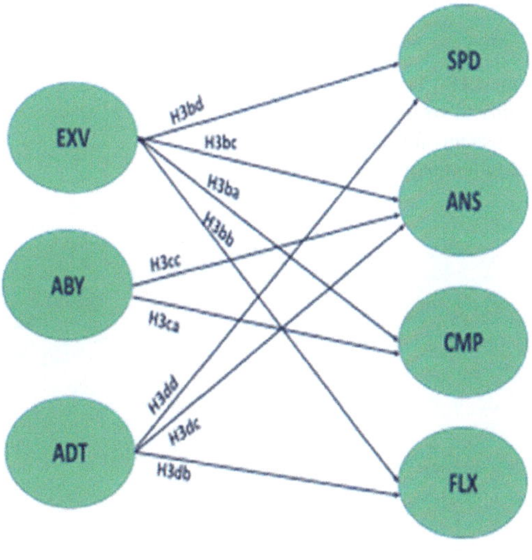

Fig. 4.17 The effect of organizational Ambidexterity dimensions on organizational agility dimensions

Political leadership; aims to integrate with many parties, both inside and outside the organization, such as business partners, employees, customers, suppliers, and thus to find the resources needed for the development of the organization. In this leadership structure, effective use of communication skills and negotiation skills, which play important roles both for teamwork and increasing organizational performance, are in question. For the leaders, having political skills enable them to work flexibly and effectively by facilitating their rapid adaptation to changing environmental conditions (Akyüz 2018).

In the study, it was seen that political strategic leadership directly affects all sub-dimensions (exploratory innovation, exploitative innovation, alignment, adaptability) of organizational ambidexterity. Thus; H2ca, H2cb, H2cc and H2cd hypotheses were accepted. This result obtained in our study during the pandemic period (that is, during this period that can be described as an extraordinary period) shows that, managers actually benefit from their political leadership characteristics and communication and negotiation skills both inside and outside the organization in order to overcome this difficult continuum. In this way, it can be interpreted as the managers activating the organization's ambidexterity in a balanced way (Fig. 4.18).

Managerial strategic leadership dimension directly effects only on the alignment ability of organizational ambidexterity. The related hypothesis, that is H2ac, was accepted. Managerial leadership, in general, is a form of leadership focusing on activities aimed at maintaining the current structure of the organization and does not ring the changes unless demand is received. However, when it feels obliged to be more effective as a result of external pressures, it changes and works towards the sustainability of the organization in this way. It is seen that, among the managers participating in the research those who carry on management with their managerial strategic leadership characteristics prefer to intervene only when it is necessary to adapt to the conditions in order to ensure sustainability (Fig. 4.19).

Even though the managerial leadership has no direct effect on organizational agility, it has been observed that organizational agility has an indirect effect

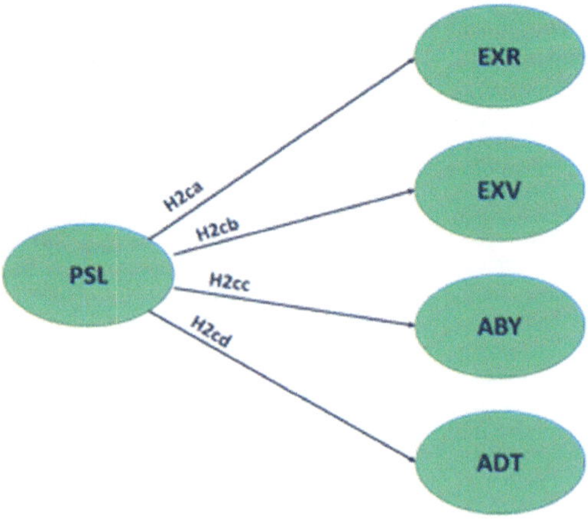

Fig. 4.18 The effect of political strategic leadership on organizational ambidexterity

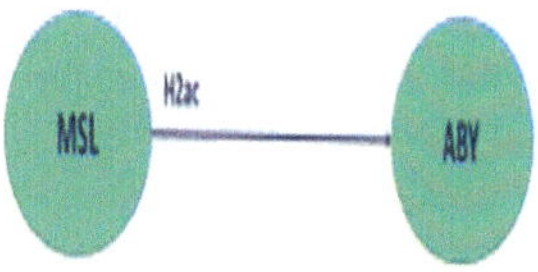

Fig. 4.19 The effect of managerial strategic leadership on organizational ambidexterity dimensions

on competence dimension (H4aa) and responsiveness dimension (H4ac) through organizational ambidexterity. Two related hypotheses were accepted (Fig. 4.20).

It is seen that organizational ambidexterity has a positive mediating effect between political strategic leadership and organizational agility (Table 4.21). In other words, political leadership does not have a direct effect on organizational agility, but it affects all dimensions of organizational agility through organizational ambidexterity. Hypotheses regarding the mediating effect of organizational agility in the dimensions of competence (H4ca), flexibility (H4cb), responsiveness (H4cc), and speed (H4cd) were accepted (Fig. 4.21).

In our study, it was understood that communicative strategic leadership and transformational strategic leadership had no direct effect on any of the sub-dimensions of organizational ambidexterity. On the other hand, the effects of ethical strategic leadership on the dimensions of organizational ambidexterity yielded unexpected results. It has been observed that ethical strategic leadership has a direct but negative effect on exploitative, adaptation and adaptability from organizational ambidexterity dimensions. Therefore, the relevant hypotheses were rejected.

According to the analysis results of our study, despite all hypotheses about ethical strategic leadership are rejected, it is thought that a comment is needed. In the study, it is understood that ethical strategic leadership has a negative direct effect on all dimensions of organizational ambidexterity. Besides, it is seen that ethical strategic leadership does not have a negative direct effect on organizational agility, but has a negative effect in all dimensions through organizational ambidexterity. In this particular, a comment can be made on the five ethical scenarios determined by Banerji and Krishnan (2000). The topics that their scenarios focused on were: 1. Bribery, 2. Endangering the physical environment, 3. Lying, 4. Personal gain, and 5. Nepotism. The selection was made by the researchers considering these situations as the most common ethical dilemmas worldwide. As Banerji and Krishnan (2000) stated

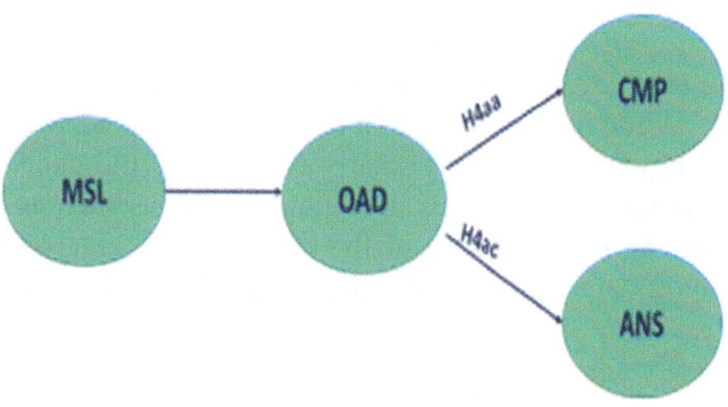

Fig. 4.20 The effect of managerial strategic leadership on organizational agility through organizational ambidexterity

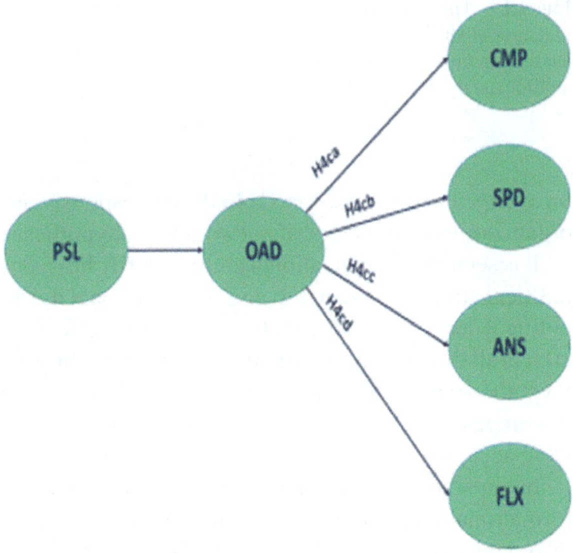

Fig. 4.21 The effect of political strategic leadership on organizational agility through organizational ambidexterity

in their work, a situation that centers the physical environment can lead to ethical dilemmas in today's corporate world, where environmental issues are not yet prioritized and default on such issues rarely leads to strict penalties. Similarly, considering the duration of legal proceedings and the complexities of the legal system, the level of ethical beliefs of the person ultimately determines the behavior.

There was no study conducted on the ethical scenarios mentioned in our study, but considering these issues, when the results related to ethical strategic leadership came in sight, in our interviews with the automotive, informatics and service sector senior executives we asked them to evaluate this result. All of the managers addressed similar issues and stated that "*long and multi-stage legal procedures, especially in the procurement processes, slowed things down, that is, this situation weakened them in being fast, they could not act flexibly, and this situation put their organizations at a competitive disadvantage in meeting the expectations of the customers*". They expressed that "*in such cases, it is necessary to make quick decisions so that the company does not get into a difficult situation, and when ethical dilemmas are encountered, they want to act in the direction of continuing the activities by taking responsibility individually, but they apply the procedures because the ethical rules in their organizations are strict, and this affects organizational agility negatively*".

While it is accepted that it is important to act according to ethical strategic leadership behaviors, particularly considering the pandemic period, the difficulties in coping with these new changing conditions such as difficulties in providing input, coming to a standstill of the production in enterprises, increase in the number of layoffs of employees, the shift of competition to the digital environment, show that leaders have difficulties in making decisions. Participants evaluate that their efforts on exploratory, exploitative, adaptation and adaptability are unsuccessful to the extent that they strictly adhere to ethical rules in organizational ambidexterity efforts carried out in enterprises.

In addition, it was determined that there is a relationship between competency and flexibility at the level of 0.52, a relationship between competency and responsiveness at the level of 0.80, and a relationship between competency and quickness at the level of 0.65. Similarly, there is a relationship between flexibility and responsiveness at the level of 0.54, and a relationship between flexibility and quickness at the level of 0.36. Likewise, it is seen that there is a relationship between responsiveness and quickness at the level of 0.67. The compatibility of sub-dimensions in organizational agility to support each other will positively affect the expected organizational performance results. We can say that the increase in the competencies of the employees and the organization in general interacts with other dimensions of agility such as flexibility, responsiveness to expectations and speed. It is an expected case that the increase in the competencies of the companies and the increase in the rapid response skills will be in the same direction and at a high level, and it is also seen that the highest level of relationship is between these dimensions.

Acknowledgements I would like to thank Prof. Dr. Adil Oguzhan, Head of Econometry Department, Faculty of Economics and Business Science, Trakya University, for his support during the analysis of the data of my research.

References

Akkaya B, Tabak A (2018) Örgütsel Çeviklik Ölçeğinin Türkçeye Uyarlanması: Geçerlik ve Güvenirlik Çalışması. İş ve İnsan Dergisi. Yıl 2018, Cilt 5, Sayı 2, 185–206. https://doi.org/10.18394/iid.439184

Akyüz M (2018) Stratejik Liderlik. Stratejik Yönetim Araştırmaları Dergisi , 1 (1):45–66 . Retrieved from https://dergipark.org.tr/tr/pub/syad/issue/36377/357631

Arokodare MA, Asikhia OU (2020) Strategic agility: achieving superior organizational performance through strategic foresight. Global J Manage Bus Res Adm Manage 20(3). Version 1.0 Year 2020. Online ISSN: 2249-4588 & Print ISSN: 0975-5853

Aydın MK (2012) Kamu ve özel ilköğretim okulu müdürlerinin stratejik liderlik özellikleri ile kurumların örgütsel öğrenme düzeyleri arasındaki ilişki. Yüksek Lisans Tezi. Gazi Üniversitesi Eğitim Bilimleri Enstitüsü, Ankara

Bakan İ, Erşahan B, Büyükbeşe T, Soğancı G (2019) Örgütsel Ustalığın, Kurumsal İmaj ve Kurumsal İtibar Üzerindeki Etkisi: Bir Alan Araştırması. Yönetim ve Ekonomi Araştırmaları Dergisi. Cilt: 17 Sayı:2 Haziran.ss.193–213. https://doi.org/10.11611/yead.506840

Banerji P and Krishnan VR (2000) Ethical preferences of transformational leaders: an empirical investigation. Leadersh Org Dev J. https://doi.org/10.1108/01437730010358161

Bayram N (2010) Yapısal Eşitlik Modellemesine Giriş. AMOS Uygulamaları. Ezgi Kitabevi. s: 51. ISBN: 978-975-8606-89-4. 978-1-4619-2882-9

Byrne BM (2010) Structural equation modeling with AMOS. In: Basic concepts, applications and programming, 2nd edn. Routledge. Taylor & Francis Group, New York

Clauβ T, Kraus S, Kallinger FL, Bican PM, Brem A, Kailer N (2020) Organizational ambidexterity and competitive advantage: The role of strategic agility in the exploration-exploitation paradox. J Innov Knowl. https://doi.org/10.1016/j.jik.2020.07.003

Crocitto M, Youssef M (2003) The human side of organizational agility. Ind Manag Data Syst 103(6):388–397

Çekmecelioğlu HG, Günsel A, İlhan ÖÖ (2018) Keşifsel ve Geliştirici Yeteneğe Dayalı Çift Yönlülük: Dönüşümcü Liderlik, Çift Yönlülük, Firma Yenilikçiliği Arasındaki İlişkileri İncelenmesi. Bus Econ Res J 9(1):137–150

Çokluk Ö, Şekercioğlu G, Büyüköztürk Ş (2012) Sosyal Bilimler İçin Çok Değişkenli İstatistik SPSS ve LISREL Uygulamaları, Pegem Akademi, 2.Baskı

Demiralay T (2014) Hekimlerde Örgütsel Sessizliğin Yapısal Eşitlik Modeli İle İncelenmesi. Trakya Üniversitesi SBE İşletme ABD. Yayınlanmamış Doktora Tezi. Edirne

Fu W, Deshpande SP (2014) The impact of caring climate, job satisfaction, and organizational commitment on job performance of employees in a China's insurance company. J Bus Ethics 124(2):339–349. https://doi.org/10.1007/s10551-013-1876-y

Gibson CB, Birkinshaw J (2004) The antecedents, consequences and mediating role of organizational ambidexterity. Acad Manage J 47(2):209–226

Gürbüz S (2019) AMOS ile Yapısal Eşitlik Modellemesi. Seçkin Yayınları, Birinci Baskı, Ankara. ISBN 978 975 02 5537 3

Harsch K, Festing M (2020) Dynamic talent management capabilities and organizational agility—a qualitative exploration. Hum Resour Manage 59:43–61. http://thestrategicleader.org/content/principles-strategic-leadership-0 About The SLQ. Accessed on 22 May 2020

İleri Y, Soylu Y (2014) Bir Rekabet Üstünlüğü Aracı Olarak Çeviklik Kavramı Ve Örgüt Yapısına Olası Etkileri. Selçuk Üniversitesi Sosyal Bilimler Meslek Yüksekokulu Dergisi 13(1–2):13–28 Retrieved from https://dergipark.org.tr/tr/pub/selcuksbmyd/issue/11301/135066

Jansen JJP, Van den Bosch FAJ, Volberda HW (2006) Exploratory innovation, exploitative innovation and performance: effects of organizational antecedents and environmental moderators. Manage Sci 52:1661–1674. https://doi.org/10.1287/mnsc.1060.0576

Kanste O, Miettunen J, Kyngäs H (2006) Factor structure of the Maslach Burnout Inventory among Finnish nursing staff. Nurs Health Sci 8(4):201–207. https://doi.org/10.1111/j.1442-2018.2006.00283.x

Karagöz Y (2019) SPSS AMOS Meta Uygulamalı İstatistiksel Analizler. Güncellenmiş 2. Basım. Nobel Akademik. Ankara. ISBN 978-605-320-547-0

Kline RB (2019) Yapısal Eşitlik Modellemesinin İlkeleri ve Uygulaması. Principles and practice of structural equation modelling. Dördüncü Basımdan Çeviri (Çeviri Editörü: Sedat Şen). Nobel Yayınevi. Ankara. ISBN: 978-605-7895-39-4

Lee O, Sambamurthy V, Lim KH, Wei KK (2015) How does it ambidexterity impact organizational agility? İnforms Published Online 26(2):243–472. https://doi.org/10.1287/isre.2015.0577

Lubatkin MH, Şimşek Z, Ling Y, Veiga JF (2006) Ambidexterity and performance in small-to medium-sized firms: the pivotal role of top management team behavioral integration. J Manage 32:646. https://doi.org/10.1177/0149206306290712

Malewska K, Sajdak M (2014) The intuitive manager and the concept of strategic leadership. Management 18(2). https://doi.org/10.2478/manment-2014-0041. ISSN 1429-9321.DE GRUYTER OPEN

Meydan CH, ve Şeşen H (2015) Yapısal Eşitlik Modellemesi Amos Uygulamaları. Ankara: Seçkin Yayınevi. s. 37. ISBN 9786055437015

Mulla ZR, Krishnan VR (2009) Do transformational leaders raise followers to levels of morality? Validating JamesMacGregor burns' hypothesis in the Indian context using karma-yoga. ASAC, conference: proceedings of the annual conference of the Administrative Sciences Association of Canada At: Niagara Falls (Ontario)

Oyedijo A (2012) Strategic agility and competitive performance in the Nigerian telecommunication industry: an empirical investigation. Am Int J Contemp Res 2(3):227–237

Pisapia JR (2006) Mastering change in a globalizing world: new directions in leadership. ISBN-13: 978-962-8077-00-7, ISBN-10: 962-8077-00-7. Faculty of Education Hong Kong Institute of Educational Research. The Chinese University of Hong Kong

Pisapia JR (2009) The strategic leader: new tactics for a globalizing world. ISBN 978-1-60752-152-5(pbk). ISBN 978-1-60752-153-2 (hardcover). IAP-Information Age Publishing. Inc. USA

Pisapia JR, Ying L (2011) Values and actions: an exploratory study of school principals in the mainland of China. Front Educ China 6(3):361–387. https://doi.org/10.1007/s11516-011-0137-z. © Higher Education Press and Springer-Verlag

Politis JD (2004) Transformational and transactional leadership predictors of the 'stimulant' determinants to creativity in organisational work environments. Electron J Knowl Manag 2(2):23–34

Raisch S, Birkinshaw J (2008) Organizational ambidexterity: antecedents, outcomes, and moderators. J Manage 34(3):375–409. https://doi.org/10.1177/0149206308316058. http://jom.sagepub.com/cgi/content/refs/34/3/375

Rigby DK, Sutherland J, Takeuchi H (2020) Çevikliği kucaklamak, Yönetimi dönüştüren süreçte nasıl ustalaşırsınız? Harvard Bus Rev. Kasım, 5–11 https://hbrturkiye.com/blog/e-kitap-cevik-donusume-hazir-misiniz. https://hbrturkiye.com/storage/doc/acm/acm-sayi-1.pdf. Accessed on 9 Feb 2021

Salih AA, Alnaji L (2014) Impact of strategic thinking and strategic agility on strategic performance: a case study of Jordanian insurance industry companies. Int Rev Manage Bus Res 3(4)

Saruhan ŞC, Özdemirci A (2013) Bilim, Felsefe ve Metodoloji. s.203. Beta Yayınları. İstanbul. ISBN 978-605-333-019-6

Sharifi H, Zhang Z (1999) A methodology for achieving agility in manufacturing organisations: an introduction. Int J Prod Econ 62(1):7–22

Sinha S (2015) The exploration-exploitation dilemma: a review in the context of managing growth of new ventures. Vikalpa. J Decis Makers 40(3). https://doi.org/10.1177/025609091559970

Smith WK, Tushman ML (2005) Managing strategic contradictions: a top management model for managing innovation streams. Organ Sci 16:522–536

Staub S, Arslan A (2017) Does environmental uncertainty moderate the effects of theory x and theory y leadership styles on ambidextrous innovation? J Entrepreneurship Innov Manage 6(1)

Teece DJ (2009) Dynamic capabilities and strategic management: organizing for innovation and growth. Oxford University Press. ISBN 978-0-19-954512-4. Accessed on 25 Apr 2021

Teece DJ, Pisano G, Shuen A (1997) Dynamic capabilities and strategic management. Strateg Manage J 18(7):509–533

Tushman ML, Romanelli E (1985) Organizational evolution: A metamorphosis model of convergence and reorientation. Res Org Behav

Ural A, Kılıç İ (2005) Bilimsel Araştırma Süreci ve SPSS İle Veri Analizi. s. 253. Detay Yayıncılık.Ankara. ISBN 975-8969-17-X

Ustasüleyman T (2008) Çevikliğin İşletme Performansına Etkisine Yönelik Yapısal Bir Model Önerisi. Gazi Üniversitesi İktisadi ve İdari Bilimler Fakültesi Dergisi 10(2):161–178

Veisch S, Shiri A, Eghbali N (2014) A study on ranking the effects of transformational leadership style on organizational agility and mediating role of organizational creativity. Manage Sci Lett 4:2121–2128. https://doi.org/10.5267/j.msl.2014.8.006

Wanasida AS, Bernarto I, Sudibjo N, Pramono R (2021) Millennial transformational leadership on organizational performance in Indonesia fishery startup. J Asian Financ Econ Bus 8(2):0555–0562. https://doi.org/10.13106/jafeb.2021

Wang CJ, Tsai H, Tsai M (2014) Linking transformational leadership and employee creativity in the hospitality industry: the influences of creative role identity, creative self-efficacy, and job complexity. Tour Manage 40:79–89. https://doi.org/10.1016/j.tourman.2013.05008

Werner C, Schermelleh-Engel K (2009) Structural equation modeling: advantages, challenges, and problems. In: Introduction modeling with LISREL. Goethe University, pp 1–4. Frankfurt

Weston R, Gore PA (2006) A brief guide to structural equation modeling. Couns Psychol 34(5):719–751

Xiaoyan W, Dapeng Y, Yan Y (2015) Ambidexterity in entrepreneurship: a perspective of dynamic capability. In: 2015 international conference on computational intelligence and communication networks (CICN), pp 1460–1463. https://doi.org/10.1109/CICN.2015.282

Yaşlıoğlu M (2017) Sosyal Bilimlerde Faktör Analizi ve Geçerlilik: Keşfedici ve Doğrulayıcı Faktör Analizlerinin Kullanılması. İstanbul Üniversitesi İşletme Fakültesi Dergisi, 74–85. Retrieved from https://dergipark.org.tr/tr/pub/iuisletme/issue/32177/357061

Yıldız D, Uzunsakal E (2018) Alan Araştırmalarnda Güvenilirlik Testleinin Karşılaştırılması ve Tarımsal Veriler Üzerine Bir Uygulama. Uygulamalı Sosyal Bilimler Dergisi. Sayı 1.s:14–28. https://dergipark.org.tr/tr/download/article-file/507218. Accessed on 02 May 2021

Zhou J, Bi G, Liu H, Fang Y, Hua Z (2018) Understanding employee competence, operational IS alignment, and organizational agility—an ambidexterity perspective. Inf Manage 55(6):695–708. https://doi.org/10.1016/j.im.2018.02.002

Zhu Y, Liu C, Guo B, Zhao L, Lou F (2015) The impact of emotional intelligence on work engagement of registered nurses: the mediating role of organisational justice. J Clin Nurs 24(15–16):2115–2124. https://doi.org/10.1111/jocn.12807l

Appendix A

Questionnaire Form

Dear Respondent,

The questionnaire form below has been prepared in accordance with the purpose of the research, to be used in a scientific research. The information obtained will only be used for scientific purposes and will be kept strictly confidential. In the publications that will be generated from the data will not contain any information pointing out your identity or company name. Therefore, please do not write your name. Answering the questionnaire may take about 10 minutes of yours. The completeness of your answers to the questions is extremely important for the study to achieve its purpose. If you have any questions regarding the study, please do not hesitate to contact us.

Thank you for your participation and support, I wish you good work.

Assoc. Prof. Dr. İlknur KUMKALE
Trakya University
Faculty of Economics and Administrative Sciences Department of Business Administration
Management and Organization Department
E-mail: ilknurkumkale@trakya.edu.tr
Mobile: 0.........................

1. Your Gender : Female ( ) Male ( )
2. Your Age :
3. Your Education Level
   Primary School : ( )
   Middle School : ( )
   High School : ( )
   Associate Degree : ( )
   Bachelor's Degree : ( )
   Postgraduate Degree : ( )
   Doctorate Degree : ( )

İ. Kumkale, *Organizational Mastery*, Accounting, Finance, Sustainability, Governance & Fraud: Theory and Application, https://doi.org/10.1007/978-981-16-7582-9

4. Your tenure in this company
   0–5 years : ( )
   6–10 years : ( )
   11–15 years : ( )
   16–20 years : ( )
   More than 20 years : ( )

5. Your tenure in this profession
   0–5 years : ( )
   6–10 years : ( )
   11–15 years : ( )
   16–20 years : ( )
   More than 20 years : ( )

6. Your title in this company
   Senior level manager : ( )
   Middle level manager : ( )
   Junior level manager : ( )
   Company owner /shareholder : ( )
   Other : ( )

7. Sector in which your company operates
   Manufacturing sector : ( )
   Service industry : ( )
   Commerce sector : ( )

8. Size of your company
   Micro-enterprise ( ) Small-scale enterprise ( ) Medium-scale enterprise ( ) Large-scale enterprise ( )

9. Number of in-service activities related to your profession
   1–5 ( ) 6–10 ( ) 11–15 ( ) 16–20 ( ) 21+ ( )

Strategic leadership						
Please indicate your level of agreement with the following statements by ticking (X) the most appropriate option, considering your managers in the institution you work for. **Please do not tick what should be**		Strongly disagree	Disagree	Neither agree nor disagree	Agree	Strongly agree
1	Decides how things should be done	1	2	3	4	5
2	Enforces rules and policies	1	2	3	4	5
3	Holds us responsible for meeting our obligations	1	2	3	4	5
4	Controls our work	1	2	3	4	5
5	Orders us to follow the chain of command	1	2	3	4	5

(continued)

(continued)

Strategic leadership						
Please indicate your level of agreement with the following statements by ticking (X) the most appropriate option, considering your managers in the institution you work for. **Please do not tick what should be**		Strongly disagree	Disagree	Neither agree nor disagree	Agree	Strongly agree
6	Encourages us to develop our leadershipskills	1	2	3	4	5
7	Encourages employees to adopt the organization's long-term goals	1	2	3	4	5
8	Helps us be aware of opportunities	1	2	3	4	5
9	Strives to create a common vision	1	2	3	4	5
10	Emphasizes the core values of our organization in our discussions and decision-making processes	1	2	3	4	5
11	Willing to negotiate to get works done	1	2	3	4	5
12	Ready to compromise to get help when needed	1	2	3	4	5
13	In resolving conflicts, tries to find win–win solutions (where both sides will benefit)	1	2	3	4	5
14	Gives small rewards when he/she likes the good work done	1	2	3	4	5
15	Treats people equally	1	2	3	4	5
16	Involves in an interaction with influential (reputable) people	1	2	3	4	5

(continued)

(continued)

Strategic leadership						
Please indicate your level of agreement with the following statements by ticking (X) the most appropriate option, considering your managers in the institution you work for. **Please do not tick what should be**		Strongly disagree	Disagree	Neither agree nor disagree	Agree	Strongly agree
17	Works jointly with people outside the organization	1	2	3	4	5
18	Strives to build rapport with people who may have influence on the works get done	1	2	3	4	5
19	Establishes close relationships with influential people	1	2	3	4	5
20	Uses his/her connections (like people he/she knows) and communication networks to get works done	1	2	3	4	5
21	Treat honestly with people	1	2	3	4	5
22	Encourages us to do the right thing	1	2	3	4	5
23	Respects our views and takes our views into account	1	2	3	4	5
24	Respects people's private life (privacy)	1	2	3	4	5
25	Puts the interests of the organization ahead of his/her own interests	1	2	3	4	5

Organizational ambidexterity						
Please interpret the statements by considering the company you work in and mark (X) with the way that best expresses the current situation. **Please do not tick what should be**		Strongly disagree	Disagree	Neither agree nor disagree	Agree	Strongly agree
1	Our company also responds to requests other than our current products and services	1	2	3	4	5
2	Our company invents new products and services	1	2	3	4	5
3	Our company tries new products and services in our local market	1	2	3	4	5
4	In our company, our completely new products and services are commercialized	1	2	3	4	5
5	Our company frequently evaluates new opportunities in new markets	1	2	3	4	5
6	Our company uses new distribution channels regularly	1	2	3	4	5
7	Our company seeks regularly new customers in new markets and strives to reach them	1	2	3	4	5
8	Our company makes frequent improvements in the presentation of our existing products and service	1	2	3	4	5
9	Our company regularly makes minor adaptations to our existing products and services	1	2	3	4	5
10	Our company puts improved products and services on our local market	1	2	3	4	5

(continued)

(continued)

Organizational ambidexterity						
Please interpret the statements by considering the company you work in and mark (X) with the way that best expresses the current situation. **Please do not tick what should be**		Strongly disagree	Disagree	Neither agree nor disagree	Agree	Strongly agree
11	Our company attaches importance to our supplies and improves the supply efficiency of our products and services	1	2	3	4	5
12	Our company increases the economies of scale in existing markets	1	2	3	4	5
13	Our company expands its services for existing customers	1	2	3	4	5
14	In our company, reducing the costs of internal processes is an important goal	1	2	3	4	5
15	The management systems in our company work consistently to support all the goals of the company	1	2	3	4	5
16	Company employees work in line with the same goals because our management systems avoid conflicting goals	1	2	3	4	5
17	The management systems in our company prevent us from wasting resources with inefficient activities of employees	1	2	3	4	5
18	The management systems in our company encourage employees to challenge outdated traditions / practices	1	2	3	4	5

(continued)

(continued)

Organizational ambidexterity						
Please interpret the statements by considering the company you work in and mark (X) with the way that best expresses the current situation. **Please do not tick what should be**		Strongly disagree	Disagree	Neither agree nor disagree	Agree	Strongly agree
19	The management systems in our company are flexible enough to allow us to respond quickly to changes in the market	1	2	3	4	5
20	Management systems in our company show rapid development in responding (response) to changes in our work priorities	1	2	3	4	5

Organizational agility						
Please interpret the statements by considering the company you work in and mark (X) with the way that best expresses the current situation. **Please do not tick what should be**		Strongly disagree	Disagree	Neither agree nor disagree	Agree	Strongly agree
1	Our company has got a strategic vision that will achieve its long-term goals	1	2	3	4	5
2	Our company has got adequate amount of and efficacious technology in accordance with the requirements of the age	1	2	3	4	5
3	Our company's product quality and as well as the service quality for this product is high	1	2	3	4	5

(continued)

(continued)

Organizational agility						
Please interpret the statements by considering the company you work in and mark (X) with the way that best expresses the current situation. **Please do not tick what should be**		Strongly disagree	Disagree	Neither agree nor disagree	Agree	Strongly agree
4	Our company aims to achieve the maximum output with the minimum input in all processes in order to achieve its goal	1	2	3	4	5
5	Our company makes high level product promotions	1	2	3	4	5
6	Our company has expert and authorized human resources	1	2	3	4	5
7	All business processes in our company are defined simply, loud and clearly	1	2	3	4	5
8	Our company attaches importance to provide and develop cooperation environment inside and outside the business	1	2	3	4	5
9	Our company has the efficiency of producing different product models	1	2	3	4	5
10	Our company has the flexibility of producing different amount of products and services	1	2	3	4	5
11	Our company has flexibility within the scope of human resources policies	1	2	3	4	5
12	Our company has the ability to respond quickly to changes in the customer's needs and preferences	1	2	3	4	5

(continued)

(continued)

Organizational agility						
Please interpret the statements by considering the company you work in and mark (X) with the way that best expresses the current situation. **Please do not tick what should be**		Strongly disagree	Disagree	Neither agree nor disagree	Agree	Strongly agree
13	Our company feels and perceives the direction of change within the scope of environmental change and holds itself in readiness for these changes	1	2	3	4	5
14	Our company's ability to adapt innovations and overcome the environmental and technology-induced changes quickly and timely is higher than its competitors	1	2	3	4	5
15	Our company is faster in production processes compared to its competitors	1	2	3	4	5
16	Our company is fast in introducing new products to the market	1	2	3	4	5
17	Our company distributes products and services to the customers quickly and on time	1	2	3	4	5

Our survey is over. Please make sure all questions are answered.
Thank you…

Appendix B

Ethics Committee Decision

Document Date and Number: 01.03.2021-26088

T.R.
RECTORATE OF TRAKYA UNIVERSITY
Social and Human Sciences Research Ethics Committee Board

Number : E-29563864-0.50.04.04-26088
Subject : Resolutions

Dear Assoc. Prof. Dr. Ilknur KUMKALE

Your application regarding the research you have done has been approved with the decision numbered 02/33 taken at the meeting of Trakya University Social and Human Sciences Research Ethics Committee dated 24.02.2021.

I kindly request you to take necessary action

Prof. Dr. Ayhan GENÇLER
Chairman

Annex: Ethics Committee Decision

İ. Kumkale, *Organizational Mastery*, Accounting, Finance, Sustainability, Governance & Fraud: Theory and Application, https://doi.org/10.1007/978-981-16-7582-9

This document is signed with a secure electronic signature

Document Verification Code :*BE6EKYERA* Pin Code :51722 Document Tracking Address:
https://ebys.trakya.edu.tr/enVision/Validate_Doc.aspx?

Address : Trakya Üniversitesi Rektörlüğü Balkan Yerleşkesi 22030 Edirne
Telephone : 2842234004 Faks : 2842234203
e-Mail: ozelkalem@trakya.edu.tr Web:http://www.trakya.edu.tr/
Kep Address (Registered Electronic Mail Address): trakyauni@hs01.kep.tr

For Information : Ceyda DURSUN
Title : Secretary

This document is signed with a secure electronic signature in accordance with 5th Article of 5070 Numbered Electronic Signature Law

T.R
TRAKYA UNIVERSITY
SOCIAL AND HUMAN SCIENCES RESEARCH ETHICS COMMITTEE

Number of Session: 2021/02
DECISION NO: 2021.02.33 Decision Date: 24.02.2021

The research file titled "Organizational Mastery" submitted by Our University's Faculty of Economics and Administrative Sciences Faculty Member, Assoc. Dr. Ilknur KUMKALE to Trakya University Social and Human Sciences Research Ethics Committee for evaluation was examined. It is unanimously/~~majority~~ concluded that there is no inconvenience in terms of ethical scientific standards in conducting of the research.

<table>
<tr><td colspan="2"><Signature>
Prof. Dr. Ayhan GENÇLER
Chairman
Is related to the research Yes [ ] No [X]
Attended to meeting Yes [X] No [ ]</td></tr>
<tr><td><Signature>
Prof. Dr. Rıdvan CANIM
Member
Faculty of Literature
Is related to the research Yes [ ] No [X]
Attended to meeting Yes [X] No [ ]</td><td>Prof. Ahmet Hamdi SEZER
Member
State Conservatory
Is related to the research Yes [ ] No [ ]
Attended to meeting Yes [ ] No [X]</td></tr>
<tr><td></td><td><Signature></td></tr>
</table>

Prof. Melihat TÜZÜN Member Faculty of Fine Arts Is related to the research Yes [ ] No [ ] Attended to meeting Yes [ ] No [X]	Prof. Dr. Cem ÇUHADAR Member Faculty of Education Is related to the research Yes [ ] No [X] Attended to meeting Yes [X] No [ ]
<Signature> Assoc. Prof. Dr. Gökhan ILGAZ Member Romany Language and Culture Research Institute Is related to the research Yes [ ] No [X] Attended to meeting Yes [X] No []	<Signature> Assoc. Prof. Dr. Ahmet Emre DAĞTAŞOĞLU Member Faculty of Theology Is related to the research Yes [ ] No [X] Attended to meeting Yes [X] No [ ]

<Signature> Assoc. Prof. Dr. Esma MIHLAYANLAR Member Faculty of Architecture Is related to the research Yes [ ] No [X] Attended to meeting Yes [X] No []	Assoc. Prof. Dr. Emre ATILGAN Member Project Coordination Application and Research Center Is related to the research Yes [ ] No [ ] Attended to meeting Yes [ ] No [X]
<Signature> Assoc. Prof. Dr. Hakkı Mevlüt ÖZCAN Member Career Application and Research Center Is related to the research Yes [ ] No [X] Attended to meeting Yes [X] No []	Dr. Academic Member Levent DOĞAN Member Social Sciences Institute Is related to the research Yes [ ] No [ ] Attended to meeting Yes [ ] No [X]

<Signature> Dr. Academic Member Ayşegül KILIÇ Member Balkan Research Center Is related to the research Yes [ ] No [X] Attended to meeting Yes [X] No []	

Index

A
Adaptability, 1, 10, 13–15, 29, 37, 44, 45, 62, 64, 65, 83, 86, 88, 91, 100, 103, 105–108
Adaptability ability, 14
Agility, 2, 24, 29, 37–40, 42, 47, 54, 56–58, 100, 103, 104, 109
Alignment, 1, 10, 13–15, 62, 65, 83, 85, 88, 100, 103, 105, 106
Alignment ability, 14, 64, 103, 106
Ambidextrous, 4, 16, 17, 19, 56, 100
Ambidexterity, 1, 2, 4, 5, 7–10, 12, 13, 15–19, 42, 54, 56, 64, 65, 100, 103–106
Analysis, 9, 16, 28, 46, 56, 59, 63, 66, 69, 74, 77, 79, 82, 90, 91, 96, 103, 107
Assumptions, 57, 63, 66, 90
Authority, 11, 12, 14, 42, 43, 47

B
Bartering, 29, 61
Bonding, 29, 61
Bridging, 29, 61

C
Capability, 1, 4, 5, 7, 8, 10, 13, 19, 40, 41, 44, 58
Change, 2, 3, 6–8, 11, 14–17, 19, 23–26, 29, 30, 32, 37–39, 42–49, 54–58, 73, 79, 81, 91, 105, 106, 119–121
Communicative, 33, 34, 61, 64, 71
Communicative strategic leadership, 2, 33, 61, 65, 66, 88, 107
Company, companies, 2, 3, 5–17, 19, 33, 37–40, 44–50, 53–60, 67–69, 71, 73, 74, 78–82, 100, 105, 108, 109, 113, 114–121
Competency, competencies, 2–4, 7–9, 11, 16, 18, 19, 24, 37, 39–47, 50, 54, 55, 58, 62, 64, 65, 66, 83, 87, 88, 91, 96, 100, 103, 104, 105, 107, 109
Competitive, 2, 26, 39, 40, 48, 55, 57, 58, 104, 105, 108
Competitive advantage, 1–3, 7, 9, 11, 16, 17, 24, 39, 40, 43–48, 50, 54, 55, 57, 100, 105
Contextual ambidexterity, 13–15, 18, 56, 61, 62, 105
Coordination, 9, 12, 42, 43
Covid-19 pandemic, 37, 38, 48, 49, 60, 96
Crisis, 3, 4, 37, 38, 45, 48, 49

D
Demographical characteristics, 67, 68
Descriptive statistics, 69–71, 73, 75, 78, 80
Dimensions, 1, 2, 9, 24, 29, 30, 37, 43, 44, 61, 62, 71, 77, 82–87, 90, 91, 93, 95, 96, 104–107, 109
Direct effects, 93, 95–97, 106, 107
Dynamic capabilities, 1, 38, 54, 55

E
Effects, 2–4, 7, 9, 42, 45, 47, 49, 54, 57, 58, 63–65, 84, 90, 95, 96, 103–108
Enterprises, 1, 2, 12, 16, 17, 23, 39, 40, 43, 55, 57–60, 67–69, 100, 105, 108, 109

İ. Kumkale, *Organizational Mastery*, Accounting, Finance, Sustainability, Governance & Fraud: Theory and Application, https://doi.org/10.1007/978-981-16-7582-9

Environment, 1–4, 8, 11, 15, 17, 23, 24, 25, 30, 34, 39–42, 44, 46–49, 55, 56, 58, 80, 104, 107, 108, 120
Ethical, 19, 32, 33, 56, 57, 61, 64, 82, 107–109
Ethical strategic leadership, 2, 32, 65, 66, 71, 83, 88, 96, 107, 108
Ethics, 23, 24, 29, 60
Exploitation, 1, 4–7, 9–13, 16–19, 105
Exploitative, 11, 18, 32, 54, 56, 61, 64, 65, 83, 85, 88, 91, 100, 103, 105–108
Exploration, 1, 4, 5, 7, 10–13, 16–19, 105
External, 2–4, 8, 9, 16, 24, 30, 34, 41, 45, 47, 49, 55, 56, 58, 106

F
Factor analysis, 59, 63, 69, 76, 77, 79, 83–89, 91, 92
Five dimensional strategic leadership model, 29
Flexibility, 2, 8, 12, 14, 17, 18, 24, 37, 39, 40, 44, 45, 47, 54, 55, 58, 62, 64–66, 73, 81, 83, 87, 88, 91, 96, 103, 105, 107, 109, 120

G
Global pandemic, 4

H
Hard and soft factors, 28
Hypotheses, 62, 64, 91, 93, 95, 96, 103–107

I
Indirect effects, 96, 99–102, 106
Innovation capability, 11, 105
Internal, 2, 3, 9, 16, 24, 30, 41, 45, 47, 55, 56, 58, 73, 74, 79, 118

L
Leadership, 11, 17, 18, 24–27, 29–34, 49, 54–58, 61, 64, 75, 103, 104, 106, 107, 115

M
Management, 1–5, 7–9, 11, 12, 14–19, 23, 25, 26, 29–31, 34, 39, 40, 42, 43, 45, 49, 55, 57, 58, 67, 73, 79, 106, 118, 119
Management paradox, 8
Managerial, 3, 5, 12, 19, 23, 25, 30, 31, 56, 57, 60, 61, 67, 71, 72, 106
Managerial strategic leadership, 2, 30, 61, 64, 65, 83, 88, 103, 106, 107
Managers, 2, 5–9, 15, 17–19, 23, 24–26, 34, 47, 49, 54–58, 60, 61, 67–72, 74–77, 106, 108, 114–116
Managing, 3, 5, 8, 12, 17, 29, 30, 54, 61, 82
Market, 3, 4, 11, 12, 14, 18, 37–40, 45–49, 54–58, 78, 79, 81, 100, 104, 105, 117–119, 121
Model, 2, 3, 6, 11, 23, 26, 27, 29, 33, 44–46, 49, 57–60, 62, 63, 77, 81–84, 86–93, 98, 120
Multidimensional, 56

O
Opportunities, 1, 3, 4, 8, 9, 12, 14, 16, 19, 24, 34, 37–39, 45–49, 55, 58, 67, 75, 78, 115, 117
Organizational adaptation, 5–7, 47
Organizational agility, 2, 4, 38, 39, 44, 54, 57, 60, 62, 64, 65, 73, 80–83, 87, 88, 90–92, 95, 96, 103–109, 119–121
Organizational ambidexterity, 1, 2, 6, 8–10, 12, 16–18, 54–56, 60, 61, 64–66, 78, 79, 82, 84, 86–91, 93, 95, 96, 103–109, 117–119
Organizational competency, 18, 19
Organizational design, 5
Organizational learning, 5, 6, 40, 45
Organizational mastery, 100, 103
Organization theory, 8, 49, 50

P
Pandemic, 38, 49, 54, 106, 108
Political, 19, 25, 32, 37, 56, 57, 61, 64, 71, 82, 106, 107
Political strategic leadership, 2, 32, 61, 64–66, 83, 88, 96, 103, 106–108
Proactive, 43, 44, 46, 55, 105

Q
Quickness, 37, 46, 47, 62, 83, 87, 88, 91, 100, 109

R
Research model, 62, 66, 88, 91, 93
Resilience, 44, 48
Resource–based view, 49

Responsiveness, 2, 45, 46, 62, 64–66, 83, 87, 88, 91, 96, 103, 105, 107, 109
Results, 2, 5, 9, 11, 14, 18, 31, 33, 49, 54, 57, 58, 60, 63, 66, 69, 74, 77, 82, 84, 86, 87, 91, 93, 95, 96, 103–109
Rules, 31, 42, 43, 63, 75, 108, 109, 114

S
Scale, 31, 44, 45, 60–62, 66, 68–71, 73–79, 82–93, 95, 96, 104, 118
Sector, 14, 38, 49, 67–69, 73, 108
Skill, 1, 3–6, 9, 12–19, 23, 24, 26, 27, 30, 31, 33, 34, 37, 40, 43–50, 54–57, 75, 100, 106, 109, 115
Socio–demographical characteristics, 00
Speed, 2, 3, 23, 24, 37, 39, 40, 44, 47, 54, 58, 62, 64–66, 83, 87, 96, 103–105, 107, 109
Strategic agility, 1–3, 37–40, 45–47, 49, 54, 57, 65, 96, 105
Strategic leadership, 1, 3, 4, 19, 23–32, 54–58, 60, 61, 64–66, 70, 71, 75–77, 82–86, 88, 90, 91, 93, 95, 96, 103, 104, 114–116
Strategic leadership models, 24, 26–29
Strategic management, 1, 3, 5–9, 24, 28, 39, 55, 57, 100
Structural ambidexterity, 9, 12, 14, 15, 61, 62
Structural equation modeling, 59, 63
Structure, 3, 5, 7–9, 11–18, 23, 24, 26, 31, 34, 38, 40, 42, 43, 45–47, 49, 58, 74, 77, 79, 83–85, 87, 100, 105, 106
Sustain, 8, 17, 39

T
Talent, 2, 40, 47, 55, 56
Technological innovation, 5, 6
Testing, 66, 88
Theory, 5, 8, 23, 25, 26, 49, 50, 54, 55, 57, 83, 104
Transformational, 18, 25, 31, 32, 61, 64, 71, 104
Transformational strategic leadership, 2, 29, 31, 64, 83, 88, 104, 107
Transforming, 27, 29, 61, 82

Z
Zombie companies, 38

The manufacturer's authorised representative in the EU is Springer
Nature Customer Service Centre GmbH, Europaplatz 3, 69115 Heidelberg,
Germany. If you have any concerns regarding our products, please
contact ProductSafety@springernature.com

Printed and bound by CPI Group (UK) Ltd, Croydon, CR0 4YY
30/09/2026
02225309-0006